First Edition

Common Core
Support Coach

TARGET ▶ Reading Comprehension ④

Common Core Support Coach, Target: Reading Comprehension, First Edition, Grade 4
T227NA   ISBN-13: 978-1-62362-006-6
Cover Design: Q2A/Bill Smith   **Cover Illustration:** Scott Balmer

Triumph Learning® 136 Madison Avenue, 7th Floor, New York, NY 10016

Contents

Nonfiction

Tools

Graphic Organizers and Close Reading Worksheets

Lesson 1
Myths

Myths are very old stories that were passed down orally, or told aloud. Some myths tell the stories of how a people or culture came to be. Other myths explain something about how the world works. Some of the most famous myths are those created by the ancient Greeks and Romans. Thousands of years ago, the Greeks and Romans believed in many different gods. They, like other ancient people, believed gods controlled nature and every part of life. They told myths to explain events in nature that they did not understand, such as storms, the changing seasons, and fire. Look at this photograph of a lightning storm. How do you think people long ago explained this frightening event?

Skills Focus

The Gift of Fire

| Determine the Theme | Describe a Character |

How Coyote Brought Fire to the Animal People

| Patterns across Cultures | Plot and Setting |

How Coyote Stole Fire from the Skookums

| Compare and Contrast | Allusions to Mythology |

Practice the Skill

First Read Determine the Theme

Theme is the central idea in a story. It is an insight about life that the writer wants readers to understand. A theme is always expressed as a complete thought; for example, "It is important to always tell the truth." Good readers try to figure out the theme as they read. They do this by looking at the story details. They pay attention to how the characters act and what they say and think. They notice how the story ends. Then they ask themselves, "What message is the writer trying to send me?" Sometimes, a story can have more than one theme.

Try It Read this story. It is the beginning of an ancient Greek myth.

Atalanta was strong and clever. She ran faster than the wind and could solve any problem. Her father was a powerful king. He wanted Atalanta to be married, but she was content to race the wind and study the stars.

One day, Atalanta's father told her of his plan. "I will hold a race. The winner of the race will marry you."

Atalanta did not like this idea but quickly thought of a solution. "All right," she said. "I will run in the race. If I do not win, I will marry the man who does. But if I do win the race, I will decide my future for myself."

> Discuss > **Think about the theme, or message, of this story. What is the central idea the writer wants you to understand? Look at what you know about the characters to help you figure it out. Underline the words that tell you about the theme.**

As you read, record your answers to questions about theme on the Close Reading Worksheet on page 223.

Practice the Skill

Characters are the people, animals, or other creatures in a story. Like real people, characters think, move, and speak. Their actions (the things they do) and their words (what they say) move the story along. Good readers think about characters as they read. They see what the characters are like. They think about why characters behave as they do.

Sometimes, writers tell things about the characters directly. For example, a writer may say, "Atalanta was strong and clever. She ran faster than the wind and could solve any problem." Other times, writers reveal things about their characters indirectly, through their actions and words. Good readers pay attention to all the details about the characters.

Try It Read this story. It is the end of the myth of Atalanta.

Many men wanted to marry Atalanta, but few men wanted to run in the race. They knew that Atalanta was a very fast runner. One man, Hippomenes, asked the goddess of love for help. She gave him three golden apples.

During the race, Atalanta passed many men. Then, when Atalanta was about to run past Hippomenes, he threw down the apples. Atalanta stopped to pick them up and therefore lost the race. She was sad to have lost the race. However, she was pleased that the man who won was not only fast but also clever.

Discuss **Think about the characters in the story. What is Atalanta like? Circle the words or phrases that tell you. Put a box around the words that tell you about Hippomenes.**

As you read, complete the Character Web on page 224.

Purpose for Reading
Read along with your teacher. Each time, read for a different purpose.

First Read	Focus on determining the theme.
Second Read	Focus on describing a character.
Third Read	Focus on evaluating the story critically.

The Gift of Fire

a myth from ancient Greece

What is Prometheus like? Circle the details that tell you. Write three details about him on the **Character Web**.

1   Centuries ago, the most powerful gods lived on the highest mountain and spent their days sitting on their thrones, eating and drinking. They laughed and sang all day and rested all night. However, the god named Prometheus was different. His name meant "thinks ahead," and it suited him because he was always planning for the future. He was a god of **action**; he preferred to work hard and help others, not to just relax.

2   Prometheus felt great **sympathy** for humans whenever he visited them at the bottom of the mountain. They lived in dark caves in which they were always cold and hungry. They had little food, for they did not know how to plant crops or keep animals, and they fought with one another over the few scraps they had. Prometheus had tried to help them, but they were too fearful in his presence.

3   "They need fire, and I will bring it to them," Prometheus promised. "I will go to Zeus and make my request." Prometheus went to Zeus, the king of the gods, to ask for permission to offer fire to the people. He approached Zeus on his throne and bowed at his feet. "It is my wish to share the gift of fire with the humans," Prometheus said boldly.

4   "Never!" cried Zeus, shaking his fist in anger. "The people cannot have fire, for if they do, they will become healthy and strong. Then, someday they may have strength and cunning enough to overthrow us, and that would be a true disaster! No, it is better for everyone if the humans remain in the cold and dark." With those words, Zeus turned away from Prometheus.

5   Prometheus strode off without a word or backward glance. He knew the humans needed fire, and he would discover a way to bring it to them. He was determined to carry out his promise, and he would never give up.

What central idea do you think the author is building toward? Underline the words or lines that tell you.

What new details do you learn about Prometheus? Circle them. Write the details on the **Character Web**.

Circle the details that show that Prometheus is smart. Put a box around the details that show he refuses to give up. Write the new detail on the **Character Web**.

Does Prometheus do the right thing by disobeying Zeus? Why or why not?

6   For days, Prometheus worked on a plan, but none satisfied him. Then, while walking along the river, he saw a tall reed. It was a plant that grew to several **centimeters** above Prometheus's head. He reached up, broke off a piece, and then studied it carefully. It was lightweight but strong, and it would make a good torch. Prometheus knew that this plant would hold fire and would burn slowly and for a long time.

7   So Prometheus set out on a quest to the East, where he hoped to catch some fire from the rising sun. He walked day after day and night after night, resting very little. He traveled over mountains and sailed over seas. He faced many dangers, but when he thought of the people and their sadness, he felt determined to keep his promise, and he continued his journey.

8   Finally, Prometheus reached the edge of the earth, where the sun rises each day. It was early morning, and the sun was a glowing red ball of fire. As it ascended past Prometheus, he reached out and touched it with the tip of the reed. The reed burst into flames but then burned down to a soft glow. Carefully, Prometheus tucked the fire holder into his belt and began to retrace his steps back toward the humans.

9   On the return journey, the sea was rougher, the mountains were steeper, and Prometheus encountered many fierce beasts. He feared he would not make it home, and he wondered if Zeus had sent these troubles to prevent him from bringing fire to the people. But this thought only renewed Prometheus's strength and determination.

What message does the conflict between Prometheus and Zeus suggest?

10   When Prometheus reached the caves in which the humans lived, he called to them in an urgent voice. They were afraid, so Prometheus called again more gently. As the humans emerged from their caves, he beckoned them with a strong arm. Then he arranged a pile of sticks and used the fire still burning in the reed to set it alight.

The humans finally overcome their fear and listen to what Prometheus has to say. By doing so, they gain a lot. What does this tell you about humans?

11   At first, the people were terrified, but they soon understood that fire was a source of warmth and light. They joined hands and laughed and danced around the fire. Then they bowed before Prometheus, thanking him for this wonderful gift.

12   Prometheus had even more to teach the humans. He showed them how to save the coals to make more fires in the future and how to carry those burning coals safely to people in other villages. He demonstrated how to use smoke to **communicate** over distances and then taught them how to cook their food. With fire, they would become healthier, stronger, and braver—just as Zeus had feared.

Now that you have read the whole story, think about its theme. What is the central idea the writer wants you to understand? Underline the words or sentences that tell you.

Write one sentence on the **Character Web** that describes Prometheus in comparison to Zeus.

Connect

How does the use of fire enable humans to farm? Support your answer with evidence from the text.

13   Now Prometheus was able to teach the humans even more. He taught them how to plant seeds and harvest crops and to keep and care for animals. He helped them dig for metal in the ground and then showed them how to use the gift of fire to melt and shape it into tools.

14   Soon the humans built real homes and could leave their caves forever. Now that they had enough food and felt safe, they grew wise and caring. They continued to learn about the world. They were healthy and strong enough to challenge the gods, but they were wise enough to know it would be foolish to do so. They thanked Prometheus for their new life and for his many gifts.

15   Prometheus was content when he visited the humans. He realized that his plans for the world had finally come true. It was the beginning of a true golden age, one he trusted would last forever!

Vocabulary: Greek and Latin Roots

The **root** is the part of a word that carries its meaning. Many words in English can share the same root. Many roots come from other languages, such as Greek and Latin. For example, the words *support, export,* and *import* share the Latin root *port,* which means "to carry." You can use your knowledge of roots to figure out the meaning of unfamiliar words.

Try It Read this sentence from "The Gift of Fire."

> Prometheus felt great **sympathy** for humans whenever he visited them at the bottom of the mountain.

The Greek root *path* means "feeling." How does the context of the sentence and the definition of the root help you understand what the word *sympathy* means?

Discuss **The words *empathy* and *apathy* both share the Greek root *path*. Find these words in a dictionary. How do their definitions relate to the meaning of the root?**

The following words appear in "The Gift of Fire." Find these words in the story. Read the meaning of each root in the chart. Then use the meanings to write definitions.

Word	Root Meaning	Definition
action, p. 8	Latin *act*: do	
centimeters, p. 10	Latin *centi*: one hundred; *meter*: measure	
communicate, p. 11	Latin *communis*: common, shared	

Practice the Skill

Every culture has its own myths, but there are similar patterns in myths from different places. For example, many cultures have myths that tell how the world began or how something in nature came to be. The people of many cultures also tell stories about a hero's quest, or journey. Many myths tell about tricksters. Tricksters can be heroes or villains. They can help people, but they can also trick them. As you read myths from different cultures, look for these and other patterns.

Try It Read this Filipino myth.

> Long ago, the sky and the clouds lived close to the ground. One day, an old woman went outside to pound rice into flour. Before she began, she took off her hair comb and beads and hung them on a nearby cloud. Then she went to work. The first time she raised her rice-pounding stick into the air, it knocked against the sky. The second time she raised it, she hit the sky again. After the third time, the sky began to rise.
>
> By the time the woman had pounded the rice into a fine powder, the sky had risen far above her head. When she reached for her comb and beads, she saw that they had turned into the moon and the stars.

Discuss In many myths, the actions of ordinary people lead to the creation of extraordinary things. Underline what the woman does in this story. Put a box around what happens as a result. What does this myth explain about the world? How might a similar myth from a different culture explain the creation of the moon and stars?

As you read, record your answers to questions about patterns across cultures on the Close Reading Worksheet on page 225.

Practice the Skill

Plot is the series of events that happen in a story. All good stories have a plot that keeps the reader interested. Story plots usually follow a similar pattern. First, the author introduces a problem that a character must solve. Then, something happens. Next, something else happens. The story ends after the character has faced the problem. This is called the story's resolution. Just before the resolution, there is a turning point. That's the moment when the character makes a decision about how to face the problem, and you know that the ending of the story is coming soon.

The **setting** is the time and place in which a story's action takes place. The setting can be the past, present, or future. Stories can take place in many different locations, such as at the beach, on another planet, or in your hometown.

Try It Read this excerpt from a Tibetan myth.

It was a lovely spring day when Sheep went out to eat the tender grass in the meadow. Soon, Wolf came along and told Sheep that he was very hungry and so must eat her for dinner. Sheep begged Wolf to let her go free. She promised that when the summer was over, she would be even fatter and tastier than she was at that moment. Wolf thought a moment about Sheep's suggestion and then agreed. He would wait until summer was over to eat Sheep.

Discuss Think about the plot events. What is Sheep's problem? Circle it. How does she solve it? Double underline the words that tell you. What do you think will happen next?

As you read, complete the Plot Chart on page 226.

Purpose for Reading
Read along with your teacher. Each time, read for a different purpose.

First Read	Focus on the pattern of events.
Second Read	Focus on the plot and setting.
Third Read	Focus on evaluating the story critically.

How Coyote Brought Fire to the Animal People

adapted from a Native American myth

How is this myth similar to "The Gift of Fire"?

Who has a problem in the story? What is the problem? Write it on the **Plot Chart**.

When does the story take place? Circle words that tell you.

1   Long, long ago, the animal people were sad because they had no fire to keep them warm. They were always cold and afraid.

2   The only fire in the world flickered at the top of a mountain, where three monsters—the Skookums—guarded it. The Skookums would not share fire with anyone, for if fire got into the hands of the animal people, the world would change forever.

3   One day, Coyote the trickster visited the animal people's village. He was sly, but he was also brave and intelligent. His arrival made the animal people feel hopeful.

4   "Coyote could help us get fire," exclaimed Squirrel.

5   "Coyote might trick us instead," warned Antelope.

6   To which Frog replied, "I'd rather be cold than tricked."

7   But Coyote was kind, and he knew that fire would make the animal people happy, so he promised to help them by visiting the Skookums.

8   Coyote's journey to the top of the mountain was difficult because he faced many obstacles—sharp rocks, falling boulders, and bushes that tore at his skin. But Coyote would not go back on his promise to the animal people. He was determined to help them.

9   Coyote was brave, but even he felt timid when he reached the mountaintop and saw the Skookums for the first time. They were tall and skinny and wore bright red kerchiefs on their heads. From under the kerchiefs peered eyes both sharp and watchful. One Skookum stood near the fire while the other two did chores or slept in their tent.

10   Coyote was not one to give up easily, so he settled at the edge of the Skookums' camp to observe them. He struggled to stay awake; after all, he was tired from his long climb. Finally, at dawn, he saw something unexpected.

11   The Skookum who had kept watch over the fire all night left her post and shuffled to the tent, where her sisters slept. She stuck her head into the tent and whispered, "Sister, it is time for my sleep. Take my place at the fire."

What does Coyote do after he promises to help the animal people? Write the plot event on the **Plot Chart**.

Why do you think Coyote is smart to stay hidden and watch the Skookums?

How Coyote Brought Fire to the Animal People 17

What important event happens after Coyote returns from the mountain? Write it on the **Plot Chart**.

Based on how his sisters react to Coyote, how do you think he has treated them in the past?

12 Coyote silently counted to thirty before another Skookum came out of the tent. Coyote smiled as he realized that he had discovered a weakness in the Skookums' routine. When they changed positions, the fire was left unguarded!

13 Coyote hurried back down the mountain. Now he had to develop a plan for stealing some fire. He decided to ask his sisters, who lived nearby, for help.

14 "Please help me keep my promise to the animal people," Coyote said.

15 His three sisters were not sympathetic, and they frowned at Coyote. "If we give you a plan, you will only say that you thought of it yourself," they replied.

16 First Coyote begged, and then he got angry. When anger did not work, he threatened them. He said that he would use his special powers to cause lightning to strike and hail to fall. His sisters yelped in fear because they did not like the sound of thunder or the sharpness of hail.

17 "All right!" they cried. "We will give you a plan. But if you were really smart, you would have figured it out yourself. Instead, you make threats against your sisters, which is very shameful."

18 The sisters spoke to one another quietly for a few moments and then presented Coyote with a wonderful plan.

19   Coyote laughed to himself as he trotted back to the animal people. The plan was brilliant, and he gave himself the credit of having thought of it. *So clever am I!* he thought.

20   Back at the village, Coyote presented the plan and then listened impatiently as the animal people argued about whether it would work. Coyote explained, "Friends, of course the plan will succeed. Each of you—Antelope, Fox, Cougar, Squirrel, and Frog—has a **specific** role to play."

21   The animals, excited by Coyote's words, agreed to the plan. So, while Coyote climbed back up the mountain and waited for the sun to go down and then rise again, the animal people took their positions.

22   At dawn, Coyote watched as one Skookum shuffled over to the tent and whispered, "Sister, it is your turn." Coyote sprang into action. He dashed from his hiding place to the fire and seized a burning ember before racing away.

23   A moment later, he heard the pounding of the Skookums' feet and their shrieking voices as they ran after him. Coyote tore at the ground with his paws, kicking up dirt and rocks. He had to stay ahead of the Skookums until he reached his **destination**.

Many myths have objects or people that come in threes. How is the number three used in this story? How are the three things important?

What is the first step in Coyote's plan to steal the fire? Write your answer on the **Plot Chart**.

How Coyote Brought Fire to the Animal People   **19**

How is Coyote's quest, or effort, to bring fire to the animal people similar to or different from Prometheus's quest in "The Gift of Fire"?

How does Coyote, with the help of the other animals, solve the problem in the story? Write your answer on the **Plot Chart**.

Support

In many Native American myths, Coyote is a trickster figure—a character of great intelligence that is also capable of doing mischief. Is Coyote a trickster in this story?

24   Moments later, Coyote met Cougar, and he passed off the burning ember to the big cat. Cougar grabbed it and then leapt into the bushes. He ran so fast, he thought his heart would burst, but he finally reached Fox. Fox then took the glowing ember from Cougar and charged through the **undergrowth**.

25   Squirrel squeaked, "Over here!" and grabbed the dying ember from Fox. He skittered up a tall tree. He could hear the Skookums shrieking as they ran along the forest floor.

26   Next, Antelope took the ember, which was now barely a glowing coal, and ran to the last animal in the chain—Frog. Frog swallowed the coal and swam across the pond. He had to protect it somehow, so he spit the coal into a piece of wood. Now the fire was gone. The coal had burned out. The Skookums shook the piece of wood with rage, but there was no getting fire back. The angry Skookums **retreated** back up the mountain to protect what was left of the fire.

27   After Coyote caught his breath, he showed the animal people how to get fire out of wood—just as his sisters had told him—by rubbing two sticks together. Then he showed them how to build a tiny ember into a roaring blaze. He explained how to feed a fire and to keep it from going out. From that time on, the animal people were able to stay warm and cook their food. They were happier than they had ever been before.

Vocabulary: Using Reference Materials

A **dictionary** is a reference book that tells the definition of a word. Words are listed in alphabetical order in a dictionary. A **thesaurus** is a book of synonyms. It lists words that have similar meanings.

Try It Read this sentence from "How Coyote Brought Fire to the Animal People."

> The angry Skookums **retreated** back up the mountain to protect what was left of the fire.

The first entry below comes from a dictionary. The second entry comes from a thesaurus.

> **re•treat•ed** (ri-ˈtrēt-id) *verb.* **1:** left or went back
>
> **retreated** *verb.* returned, retired, fell back, went back, backtracked

Discuss **Think about the meaning of the word *retreated* and how the dictionary and thesaurus entries differ.**

The following words appear in "How Coyote Brought Fire to the Animal People." Check a dictionary and a thesaurus. Then write the definition and a synonym for each word.

1. **specific,** p. 19 _____

2. **destination,** p. 19 _____

3. **undergrowth,** p. 20 _____

Practice the Skill

First Read **Compare and Contrast**

When you compare and contrast two or more things, you consider how they are similar and different. You **compare** by thinking about how things are alike and by using words such as *similar, same, and,* or *like.* You **contrast** by thinking about how things are different and by using words such as *but, different,* or *unlike.* Comparing and contrasting will help you better understand what you read.

Try It Read this myth.

> Poseidon was a sea god. His niece Athena was the goddess of wisdom. Both wanted a village named in his or her honor. In order to persuade the villagers, they each gave the village a gift. Poseidon threw his staff on the ground, and a stream of water gushed forth. The villagers were delighted until they realized the water was salty seawater. They could not drink it! Then Athena waved her hand, and an olive tree appeared. The villagers were pleased. Olive trees would provide food, oil, and shelter from the sun. They made Athena their patron, or protector, and called their village Athens, which became the center of a great kingdom.

> Discuss **How are Athena and Poseidon similar and different? Underline the things the two characters have in common. Double underline their differences.**

> **As you read, record your answers to compare and contrast questions on the Compare and Contrast Chart on page 227.**

Practice the Skill

An **allusion** is a word or phrase that refers to a well-known story or event. Authors use allusions to make their writing more interesting. Many allusions refer to mythology. Because myths are well-known, readers are likely to understand allusions to them. For example, you can guess what a *Promethean* character is like. He or she is a bold and creative person—like Prometheus, who gave people the gift of fire against Zeus's wishes.

Try It Read this myth.

> Hercules was the strongest man in the world. One day, the goddess Hera tricked him into destroying his own family. To pay for his crime, he had to complete twelve nearly impossible tasks. One was to slay a monster called the Hydra. The Hydra had many heads, and when one was cut off, two grew back in its place. Hercules finally killed the monster and buried it under an enormous rock. Only a man of great strength could have done such a deed.

> Discuss

A writer might allude to the story of Hercules by saying, "The huge amount of work Steven had to complete would require a Herculean effort." Circle details in the myth that show the meanings of the word.

As you read, record your answers to questions about allusions to mythology on the Close Reading Worksheet on page 228.

How Coyote Stole Fire
from the Skookums

This story is a graphic novel. Its main points are made through pictures and the characters' dialogue. How are the characters in this story similar to or different from those in "How Coyote Brought Fire to the Animal People"? Write your ideas on the **Compare and Contrast Chart.**

In Greek myth, an old man who taught a young hero was named Mentor. Why do you think Squirrel calls Coyote his mentor?

3

Coyote, we are so relieved to see you! We desperately need your help. Can you bring us fire from the mountain? We are freezing and hungry.

Squirrel, I'm always glad to help and guide you. Let me see what I can do.

How is Coyote's effort to climb the mountain here similar to the effort made by Coyote in "How Coyote Brought Fire to the Animal People"? Write the details on the **Compare and Contrast Chart.**

Why might Coyote's efforts to climb the mountain be described as *Herculean*?

4

Coyote faced a difficult task. First, he had to climb up the steep mountain. It took him many hours to do it.

Arrgh! I must keep going. I must help my friends.

5

There's the fire—and the **wicked** Skookums are guarding it!

How does Coyote come up with his plan in the first version of the story? How does he do it in the graphic novel? Write your answers on the **Compare and Contrast Chart.**

Achilles was a great warrior of Greek myth. Only one part of his body could be harmed—his heel. What is the Skookums' Achilles' heel?

Why does Coyote say his thoughts aloud here but not in the story version?

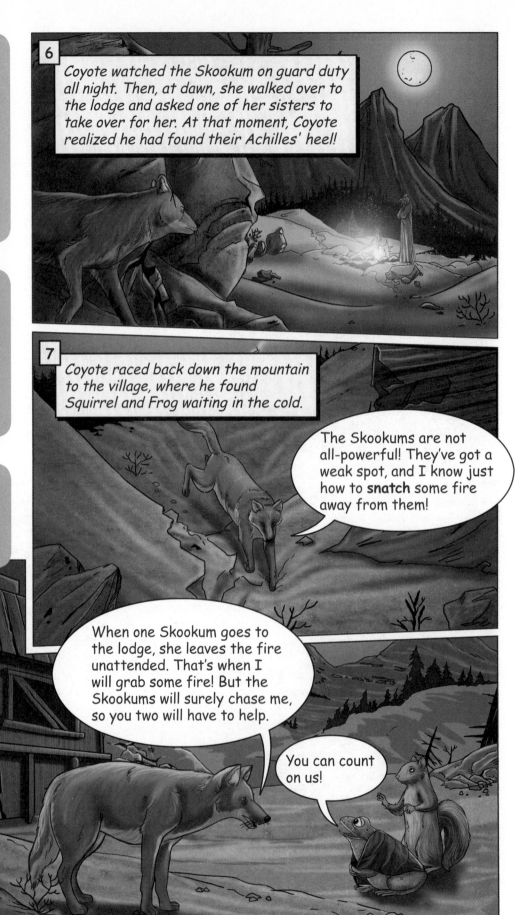

6 Coyote watched the Skookum on guard duty all night. Then, at dawn, she walked over to the lodge and asked one of her sisters to take over for her. At that moment, Coyote realized he had found their Achilles' heel!

7 Coyote raced back down the mountain to the village, where he found Squirrel and Frog waiting in the cold.

The Skookums are not all-powerful! They've got a weak spot, and I know just how to **snatch** some fire away from them!

8 When one Skookum goes to the lodge, she leaves the fire unattended. That's when I will grab some fire! But the Skookums will surely chase me, so you two will have to help.

You can count on us!

9

Late that night, Coyote scaled the mountain again and then waited patiently for his chance to steal the fire.

Aha! I've got it—the Skookums' precious fire. Now everyone can be warm.

Sisters! Coyote has stolen our fire!

How is the plan to steal fire from the Skookums here different from the plan in the story version? Write your answer on the **Compare and Contrast Chart.**

Many myths have things that come in threes. What things in this graphic novel come in threes?

10

Coyote **sped** through the night and down the mountain to the edge of the forest. The angry Skookums chased after him.

11

Here's the fire, Squirrel! Now run!

Squirrel took off through the forest, hopping from branch to branch in the treetops.

How Coyote Stole Fire from the Skookums 27

How are the endings of the story and the graphic novel similar? Write your answer on the **Compare and Contrast Chart.**

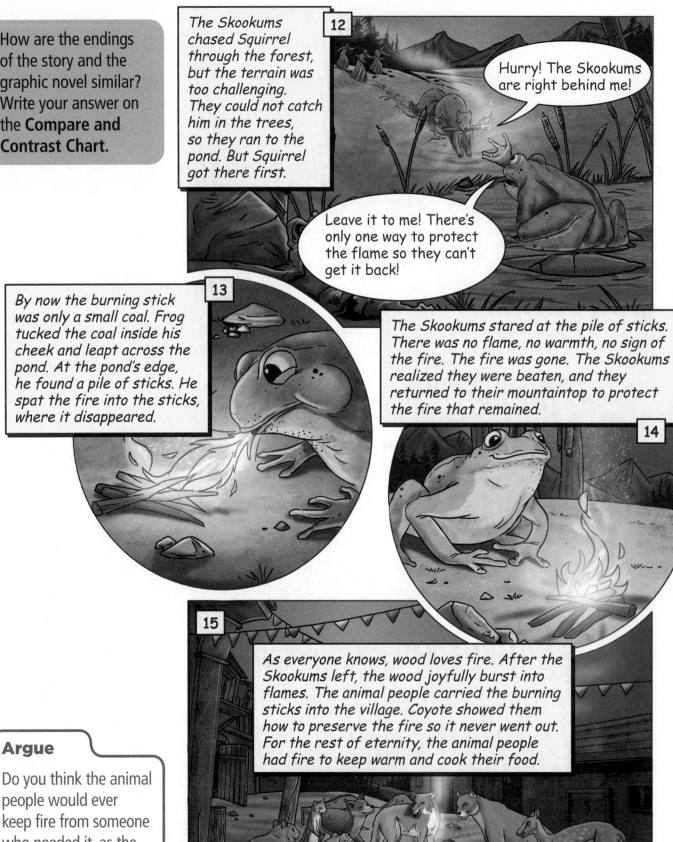

The Skookums chased Squirrel through the forest, but the terrain was too challenging. They could not catch him in the trees, so they ran to the pond. But Squirrel got there first.

12

Hurry! The Skookums are right behind me!

Leave it to me! There's only one way to protect the flame so they can't get it back!

By now the burning stick was only a small coal. Frog tucked the coal inside his cheek and leapt across the pond. At the pond's edge, he found a pile of sticks. He spat the fire into the sticks, where it disappeared.

13

The Skookums stared at the pile of sticks. There was no flame, no warmth, no sign of the fire. The fire was gone. The Skookums realized they were beaten, and they returned to their mountaintop to protect the fire that remained.

14

15

As everyone knows, wood loves fire. After the Skookums left, the wood joyfully burst into flames. The animal people carried the burning sticks into the village. Coyote showed them how to preserve the fire so it never went out. For the rest of eternity, the animal people had fire to keep warm and cook their food.

Argue

Do you think the animal people would ever keep fire from someone who needed it, as the Skookums did? Why or why not?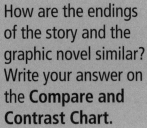

Vocabulary: Precise Language

Writers choose their words carefully so they can express their ideas precisely. Sometimes, writers have to choose among words with similar meanings. For example, the words *little, tiny,* and *petite* all mean "small," but *tiny* sounds the smallest.

Try It Read this sentence from the graphic novel.

> There's the fire—and the **wicked** Skookums are guarding it!

The writer could have used a less precise word, such as *mean*, but *wicked* makes the Skookums sound really bad.

> Discuss   **Think of other words that the writer could have used instead of *wicked*. How do they change the meaning of the sentence?**

Find the words below in the graphic novel. Then think of another word with the same meaning. Use that word in a sentence about the story.

1. **mighty,** p. 24 _____

_____

2. **snatch,** p. 26 _____

_____

3. **sped,** p. 27 _____

_____

Respond to Text: Compare and Contrast

Myths from different cultures can have similar elements. "The Gift of Fire" and "How Coyote Brought Fire to the Animal People" are myths from different cultures that tell a similar story.

Try It Think about "How Coyote Brought Fire to the Animal People." How are the events and characters in it similar to or different from those in "The Gift of Fire"?

> Discuss   **Both myths tell how people got fire, but the stories are different in several ways. Compare and contrast the two stories. Think about their elements—characters, plot events, setting, and theme. Remember to support your ideas with evidence from the stories.**

On Your Own Write a paragraph that compares and contrasts the two stories. Include details from both stories to support your ideas. Use the next page to help you plan your response. Then write your paragraph on a separate sheet of paper.

Checklist for a Good Response

A good paragraph

✔ tells the ways in which the stories are similar.

✔ tells the ways in which the stories are different.

✔ includes text evidence from both stories.

✔ shows your understanding of the stories.

✔ includes a topic sentence, supporting ideas, and a concluding statement.

My Comparison and Contrast of the Stories

1. **Topic Sentence** Include this information in your first sentence:

    The stories "The Gift of Fire" and "How Coyote Brought Fire to the

    Animal People" have similar _____

    _____ but have different _____.

2. **Detail Sentences** The sentences of your paragraph should provide
    details that show similarities and differences in the stories. Use this
    chart to organize your ideas.

	"The Gift of Fire"	**"How Coyote Brought Fire to the Animal People"**	**How the Stories Are Similar**
Culture			
Characters and Their Traits			
Plot Events			
Theme			

3. **Concluding Sentence** Your concluding sentence should restate your
    comparisons and contrasts in a new way.

    _____

    _____

On a separate sheet of paper, write your paragraph.

Read on Your Own

Read the story independently three times, using the skills you have learned. Then answer the Comprehension Check questions.

First Read Practice the first-read skills you learned in this lesson.

Second Read Practice the second-read skills you learned in this lesson.

Third Read Think critically about the story.

King Midas and the Golden Touch

Compare and Contrast As you read, think about how King Midas is similar to or different from his daughter.

Character What do you learn about King Midas's character? Circle words and phrases that reveal his character. One has been circled for you.

1   There once lived a king named Midas who loved his daughter and owned a castle full of gold. Midas loved to spend his days counting his gold, but he loved his daughter even more. Only if she asked him to stop counting his gold and to walk with her on the castle grounds would he set aside his piles of riches.

2   King Midas knew his daughter was a treasure because she was lovely and kind and had a lively sense of humor. His only wish was to provide for her future, and that meant he had to get even more gold for her **benefit**. All the gold was really only for his daughter, he told himself. It was not to feed his own sense of greed—not at all!

3   One evening, King Midas was alone in his counting room. A soldier entered with a stranger at his side. He announced that the stranger had appeared at the castle gate and insisted on seeing the king. The stranger apologized for disturbing the king, but he had an important question.

4   King Midas noticed the stranger's confidence and the gleam in his eye, which reminded him of the glow of gold. "What is it that you want?" asked the king.

5   The man said, "Sir, you are rich, but I think you are not happy. If you could make any wish, what would it be?"

6   King Midas glanced at his small piles of gold and answered, "I wish that everything I touched would turn to gold."

7   The stranger's eyes lit up. "Ah, the golden touch," he said. "It will certainly increase your riches. Will it bring you happiness?"

8   King Midas thought the question was odd. Such a power would make him the richest man in the world. That would surely bring happiness.

9   The stranger bowed and said, "Your wish is granted, my lord. In twelve hours, you will have the golden touch." As he turned to leave, he added, "I am staying at the local inn if I should be needed . . ."

10   The king dismissed him with a flick of his hand. He was already thinking about all the things he would turn into gold.

Patterns across Cultures As you read, think about how the stranger might be a trickster. What lesson might he want King Midas to learn?

Plot What problem does King Midas have? How does he solve it? Underline the sentences that tell you.

Critical Thinking Think about why the stranger asks King Midas if the gold will bring him happiness.

Theme <u>Underline</u> words or phrases that show what King Midas learns. Use them to think about the theme, or big idea, the author wants you to understand.

Allusions to Mythology Pandora is a character from Greek mythology. She opened a box from the gods that was filled with the world's troubles, unleashing them on humans. Think about how this allusion fits the story of King Midas.

Critical Thinking Think about how King Midas will act in the future. Will he change his ways, or will he still be greedy for gold?

11   The king awoke the next morning with great anticipation. He pushed back the blanket. To his amazement, it turned into a cloth of pure gold. The king happily ran around the room, turning his washbowl and bedpost and pillows into gold.

12   At breakfast, the chair King Midas touched turned **automatically** into gold, as did his napkin and fork. But then the king discovered he had opened a Pandora's box of horrors. As he touched his food and drink, it too turned into gold. He could not eat!

13   Then the king's daughter came into the room. As she threw her arms around her father, she turned into a statue of gold. As Midas brushed away his tears, they too were transformed into droplets of gold. He ordered his soldier to bring the stranger to him immediately.

14   When the stranger arrived, he said to the king, "You look unhappy."

15   The king fell to his knees and sobbed, "Please take back the golden touch. I have been a fool. I would give all my gold to bring my daughter back."

16   The stranger was satisfied that King Midas had learned an important lesson. Then he ordered the king to jump into a nearby river. The waters would wash away his golden touch. If the king sprinkled some river water over his daughter, she would return to life.

17   King Midas bowed in gratitude before the stranger and then ran to the river. He erased the golden touch. He cried when his daughter opened her eyes and laughed. From that moment on, he spent his days walking on the castle grounds with her and only rarely counted his small piles of gold.

✔ Comprehension Check

1. Compare and contrast the character of King Midas at the beginning and the end of the story. How and why does he change?

_____

_____

_____

2. What lesson does King Midas learn in this story? Write details from the story to support your answer.

_____

_____

_____

3. How is the stranger a trickster figure? Are his actions noble or mischievous or both? Support your answer with evidence from the text.

_____

_____

_____

4. Read this sentence from the story.

> **His only wish was to provide for her future, and that meant he had to get even more gold for her benefit.**

The Latin root *bene* means "good" or "well." Based on that information, what does the word *benefit* mean?

_____

_____

_____

5. Read this sentence from the story.

> **At breakfast, the chair King Midas touched turned automatically into gold, as did his napkin and fork.**

Where would you find the meaning of the word *automatically*? What is another word the author might have used instead?

_____

_____

_____

6. Reread paragraph 12 of the story. Explain the meaning of the allusion to Pandora's box.

_____

_____

_____

Lesson 2
Short Stories

A short story is a made-up piece of fiction with characters, a setting, and a plot. Unlike a novel, a short story can usually be read in one sitting and often focuses on one main character and event. A short story can be realistic, based on characters and events that are familiar and modern. Or a short story can be set in the past or even the future. Imagine reading a short story about the girl in this photo. What do you think the story might be about?

Skills Focus

Things That Go Thump in the Night

| Draw Inferences | Idioms, Adages, and Proverbs |

What Are Friends For?

| Draw Conclusions | Point of View |

Practice the Skill

An **inference** is an educated guess that you make about the characters, settings, or events in a story. An author does not always tell you everything that takes place in a story. You can use details in the story, along with your own personal knowledge and experience, to draw an inference, or figure out something that the author has not stated directly. For example, if an author writes that a boy's palms are sweaty and his heart is beating quickly, you can infer that the boy is nervous.

Try It Read this paragraph.

> Cara waited at the bus stop with three other students whom she recognized from her neighborhood. Orange and yellow leaves fluttered down around them. The wind was blowing, and Cara pulled her coat more tightly around her. Florida had been so warm. Would she ever get used to the cold?

Discuss **What do you know about the setting? Underline details in the text that you can use to make an inference about where and when this story takes place. What do you know about Cara? Double underline details in the text that help you better understand this character.**

As you read, record your answers to inference questions on the Close Reading Worksheet on page 229.

Practice the Skill

Second Read Idioms, Adages, and Proverbs

Sometimes authors include expressions, or sayings, in their writing that have meaning beyond their individual words. Three common types of expressions are idioms, adages, and proverbs. For example, the **idiom** "A penny for your thoughts" does not mean that someone is literally giving pennies in exchange for thoughts. Instead, this idiom is another way of asking someone, "What are you thinking about?"

An **adage** expresses a truth about human nature or how people behave. For example, the adage "Birds of a feather flock together" means similar people spend time with one another.

Finally, a **proverb** is an expression that gives advice about how to live your life. For example, "Do not judge a book by its cover" is a proverb that tells you not to judge people or things only by what they look like.

Try It Read these paragraphs from a short story.

> I pointed to the clock and frowned at my brother when he arrived.
>
> "Hey, better late than never!" he said.
>
> I noticed that he was trying to hide a smile. He was keeping a secret. It was as plain as the nose on his face. "Okay, spill the beans," I told him. "You know something about my party, right?"
>
> He broke into a wide smile and said, "Remember, curiosity killed the cat. You'll have to wait until tomorrow!"

Discuss **Circle the idioms, adages, and proverbs. How do the clues in the text help you figure out the meanings of the expressions? How does the meaning of each expression differ from its literal, or actual, meaning?**

As you read, complete the Idioms, Adages, and Proverbs Chart on page 230.

Purpose for Reading

Read along with your teacher. Each time, read for a different purpose.

First Read — Focus on drawing inferences about the characters and events.

Second Read — Focus on understanding idioms, adages, and proverbs.

Third Read — Focus on evaluating the story critically.

Things That Go Thump in the Night

How does Zuri feel about staying at her aunt's house? Underline details that help you infer how she feels.

What does Zuri's mom mean when she says, "Don't bite the hand that feeds you"? Add the meaning to the **Idioms, Adages, and Proverbs Chart**.

1 There's nothing like starting your fall break in the middle of a thunderstorm, maybe even the worst storm ever recorded. OK, so maybe I **exaggerate** a little and make things seem worse than they really were. But I'm telling you, the thunderstorm was fierce that night when Mom dropped me off at 1313 Blackbird Circle.

2 Lightning flashed! Thunder boomed! The wind howled around the corners of the creepy old house that belonged to my mom's older sister, Aunt Drusilla.

3 Mom had to go to Philadelphia for work, and even though I begged, she wouldn't let me come along. She mentioned something about the last time I went with her on a business trip and how I challenged her boss to a chess game and beat him.

4 How was I supposed to know that he considered himself a chess champ? The guy had no sense of strategy at all! Even Mom could have beaten him, and I told her so. She'd replied, "Now, Zuri, don't bite the hand that feeds you. Mr. Gremlik signs my paycheck."

5   OK, I understood, but that still didn't make it any easier to spend a week in that big, weird house covered with creeping vines and cobwebs. Mom said that Aunt Drusilla was just too busy to trim back the vines and knock the cobwebs off the front porch, but I think she liked it that way. After all, she did install that strange-sounding doorbell that scares anyone who dares come to her front door.

6   "Good evening, sweet Zuri!" Aunt Drusilla called out to me, reaching for my raincoat with hands that looked like bird **talons**. "This is a frightfully wicked night, wouldn't you say? It's raining cats and dogs!"

7   "It sure is, Aunt Drusilla," I replied. Lightning flashed again, casting long shadows across the ancient-looking paintings on the walls. "Mom said she was sorry she didn't have time to come in, but she had to get to the airport."

8   "Your dear mother, always running here and there!" Aunt Drusilla cackled. "Even as a child she was up at the crack of dawn to check her homework once more or to get a head start on her chores. 'The early bird gets the worm!' she used to say to me! And I would reply, 'Yes, but sometimes an early bird gets eaten up by an even earlier cat!'"

9   Aunt Drusilla laughed, leaving me to wonder what she was talking about.

10   *THUMP! THUMP! THUMP!*

11   "What was that?" I asked.

Underline the part of the text that helps you make an inference about Aunt Drusilla's character. How would you describe her?

What do the sayings "It's raining cats and dogs" and "The early bird gets the worm" mean? Add the meanings to the **Idioms, Adages, and Proverbs Chart**.

12   Aunt Drusilla dropped my raincoat. "Oh, that's nothing," she said nervously, "or perhaps it's a tree branch blowing against the house."

13   Was it my imagination, or did Aunt Drusilla seem a bit **flustered**?

14   "I imagine you'll want to get settled in your room," she said. "It's at the top of the stairs and then to the left."

15   I started to climb the creaky steps and then stopped, remembering my manners. I called back down to my aunt. "Thanks for letting me stay here," I said. "Mom said she really appreciates your help. She knows that you have better things to do than to keep an eye on me all week."

16   "Bite your tongue!" Aunt Drusilla exclaimed. "This old house gets rather lonely sometimes. It's wonderful to have you here! Now, get your rest tonight, young Zuri. Tomorrow I have a surprise for you."

17   *THUMP! THUMP! THUMP!*

18   I saw Aunt Drusilla frown and then look quickly toward the ceiling and back at me.

19   "Oh, that wind!" she laughed. "It's **doubtful** any of us will sleep tonight!"

20   I, too, had great uncertainty about sleeping, but I didn't think it was the wind that would keep me awake.

Thump Thump Thump

21   "I don't know, Aunt Drusilla, it sounded more like—"

22   Before I could come up with a description, Aunt Drusilla shooed me away and told me to have a peaceful rest. At the top of the stairs, it finally came to me. It sounded like a heartbeat! A heartbeat thumping within the walls of the house!

23   By the time I put on my pajamas and crawled into bed, I had pretty much convinced myself that the noise I'd heard was only tree branches hitting the house. But why did Aunt Drusilla look so concerned when she heard it? What did she know?

24   *THUMP! THUMP! THUMP!* There it was again! I looked up at the ceiling, as if expecting a beating red heart to fall through at any minute. I heard Aunt Drusilla in the hallway. Then I heard the opening of a creaky door, followed by footsteps that seemed to be going upstairs. Was she going into the attic? But why? And what did she mean when she said she had a surprise for me? *THUMP! THUMP! THUMP! THUMP! THUMP! THUMP!*

25   I pulled the blanket over my head, but I could not escape the thumping noise. Suddenly I remembered an important chess tip. When the other player makes a move, you should ask yourself why your **opponent** did it. Then you should think about where to move next, so you'll have the most options in the future.

26   I could either stay under the covers and make no move at all, or I could crawl out of bed and find out once and for all why Aunt Drusilla was in the attic. At least then I could learn if the thumping was just the storm . . . or something else. But at least I would know. "Nothing ventured, nothing gained," I whispered and slipped out of bed and into the dark hallway.

27   The thumping grew louder as I crept up the stairs. A sliver of light shone from the attic door.

28   *THUMP! THUMP! THUMP!*

29   "Zuri, is that you?" Aunt Drusilla called out.

What details about Zuri does the author reveal in paragraph 26? Underline them in the text. What can you infer about Zuri from these details?

What does Zuri mean by the phrase "Nothing ventured, nothing gained"? Add the meaning to the **Idioms, Adages, and Proverbs Chart.**

Why does Zuri use a chess tip to help her decide what to do? What does this tell you about her?

Based on details on this page and at the beginning of the story, infer why Zuri's mom got her a puppy.

What does Aunt Drusilla mean when she says that she "let the cat out of the bag"? Add the meaning to the **Idioms, Adages, and Proverbs Chart**.

Compare

How have Zuri's feelings about staying at Aunt Drusilla's house changed? Use details from the story to support your ideas.

30   This time the thumping I heard was the sound of my own heart. "Yes," I said, my voice sounding small and scared. "I thought I heard something." *THUMP! THUMP! THUMP!* "I definitely hear something, and it's coming from in there!"

31   "Oh, very well. Come in!" I pushed open the door and found Aunt Drusilla kneeling next to a large, gray puppy. He was lapping up water from a bowl as his wagging tail thumped wildly against the floor.

32   "He's yours!" Aunt Drusilla said. "Your mother picked him out. I was supposed to give him to you tomorrow and video the big moment and send it to her. Now I've let the cat out of the bag! Well, *dog*!"

33   "He's mine? Really?" I dropped to the floor next to the puppy, who jumped into my arms and licked my face. "I heard thumping and I thought—" I stopped. Should I tell my aunt that I thought her spooky house had a heart beating somewhere within its walls?

34   Outside the storm roared. The wind howled and thunder crashed as lightning lit up the attic. "I think I let my imagination run away with me," I admitted. The puppy jumped and thumped all around. "It was the storm, I guess. *Stormy!* That's what I'll name him!" *THUMP! THUMP! THUMP!* "See, he likes that name a lot!"

Vocabulary: Context Clues

Context clues are words located near an unknown word that can help you figure out what that word means. When you come across an unknown word, read the words and sentences around it, looking for context clues that can help you understand its meaning. Sometimes, the context clue is a definition of the unfamiliar word. Other times, a synonym or antonym of the unknown word is shown nearby.

Try It Read these sentences from "Things That Go Thump in the Night."

> There's nothing like starting your fall break in the middle of a thunderstorm, maybe even the worst storm ever recorded. OK, so maybe I **exaggerate** a little and make things seem worse than they really were.

If you do not know what the word *exaggerate* means, read the other words in the sentence. Underline the words that help you figure it out.

> Discuss **Brainstorm definitions for the word *exaggerate*.**

Find these words in the story. Look for the context clues that help you understand what each word means. Then write your own definitions of the words on the lines below.

1. **talons,** p. 41 _____

2. **flustered,** p. 42 _____

3. **doubtful,** p. 42 _____

4. **opponent,** p. 43 _____

Practice the Skill

When you **draw conclusions** as you read, you use details from the story as well as your prior knowledge and experience to form an opinion or make a decision about the text. Drawing conclusions is similar to making inferences. In both, you decide what an author means but does not state directly. The difference is that when you draw a conclusion, you also make an overall decision about what you have read.

Try It Read these paragraphs from a short story.

> "Mom, the obedience school just called," Theo said. "They can take Scrappy on Wednesday." Theo gave his Mom a long look. "Are you sure you want to do this?" he asked her. "Scrappy usually listens to me. I can teach him what he needs to know."
>
> Mrs. Kent didn't have to say a word. She just pointed. At that very moment, Scrappy came bounding into the room, thrashing Mrs. Kent's favorite shoe about as if it were a wild animal.

Discuss What conclusion can you draw from this story? Will Scrappy have to go to obedience school? Underline the details that you used to draw your conclusion.

As you read, complete the Draw Conclusions Chart on page 231.

Practice the Skill

The **point of view** is the perspective from which a story is told. First-person and third-person points of view are two of the most common.

In **first-person point of view**, the narrator is a character in the story. A story told from first-person point of view uses words such as *I*, *me*, and *we*. You learn about story events through the eyes of the narrator as he or she tells about his or her experiences.

In **third-person point of view**, the narrator is someone outside of the story. A story told from third-person point of view uses words such as *he*, *she*, *him*, *her*, and *they*. You learn about the thoughts, feelings, and actions of all the characters in the story from someone who is not part of it.

Try It Read these paragraphs.

> I read the list of chores that Mom left for me on the refrigerator and sighed. It would take me all day to finish them!

> Brad wondered if he would ever finish raking all the leaves. His friends were waiting at the soccer field. They would be angry if he missed practice.

Discuss **Circle the words in the first example that tell the point of view. Draw a box around the words in the second example that tell the point of view. Which point of view do you feel is more interesting? Why?**

As you read, record your answers to questions about point of view on the Close Reading Worksheet on page 232.

Purpose for Reading

Read along with your teacher. Each time, read for a different purpose.

First Read — Focus on drawing conclusions about the characters and events.

Second Read — Focus on identifying the point of view.

Third Read — Focus on evaluating the story critically.

What Are Friends For?

Underline the details about how Tony behaves. What conclusion can you draw about the kind of friend Tony is to Christopher? Record your conclusion and the details that support it on the **Draw Conclusions Chart**.

1   "Come on, Chris! Hit it out of the park!" Tony yelled from the stands.

2   His best friend, Christopher, stepped up to home plate amid cheers from the hometown crowd. A player hopped from foot to foot on third base, eager to dash home on Chris's hit and score the tying run. This was a big game between the hometown Cheetahs and the visiting Eagles. The Eagles had beaten the Cheetahs the last four times they played. It was time for the Cheetahs to earn back their pride.

3   The Eagles pitcher wound up and hurled the ball. The crack of Christopher's bat against the ball brought the crowd to its feet. Tony raised his hands in the air as the crowd swelled into a scream.

Circle the words that tell who is speaking in this part of the story. What does this tell you about the story's point of view?

4   "Keep going! Keep going!" he shouted, willing the ball to sail over the center fielder's head. Then the grin disappeared from Tony's face as the center fielder leapt up and snatched the ball out of the air. The crowd groaned and seemed almost to **deflate**.

5   The Eagles celebrated on the mound while the Cheetahs walked off the field, their heads down. After he grabbed his glove and bat, Christopher trudged slowly to meet Tony, his parents, and his older sister Rose by the front gate.

6   "You played your best, Chris," his mom said, **reassuring** him. "I'm proud of you."

7   "If that was my best, I should quit baseball altogether," Christopher said gloomily, kicking a stone across the parking lot.

8   Christopher's dad put his arm around his son's shoulder as they all walked to the car. "Never say that, buddy. When you lose a game, put it behind you and look ahead to the next one."

9   "Yeah, Chris," Rose said with a smirk, "you definitely want to put this game behind you."

10   Christopher's mom turned around to look piercingly at Rose. Rose knew what that look meant and scurried ahead to duck into the backseat of the car.

11   Tony nudged Christopher with his elbow, "Hey, why don't you ask your parents if they can drop you off at my house? We'll watch *Dare You to Move* and get some pizza."

12   "We've watched that movie a hundred times," Christopher groaned, rolling his eyes.

Underline the details that show how Christopher's parents treat him. What conclusion can you draw about his parents? Add the details and your conclusion to the **Draw Conclusions Chart.**

Circle Rose's reaction to her mother's piercing look. Who is telling the reader about Rose's reaction? How does this show the point of view of the story?

Underline the details about how Christopher and Tony treat each other. What conclusion can you draw about their friendship? Add the details and your conclusions to your **Draw Conclusions Chart.**

Circle the details in paragraph 18 that show Jason's feelings. What do you learn about Jason from the narrator's description?

What does Tony mean when he says "what are friends for"?

Why do you think Tony isn't talking with the other boys at this point in the story?

13 "So this will be a hundred and one," Tony said, playfully knocking Christopher's baseball cap sideways. "We'll get a pizza with all the toppings—well, except for my half, of course, because I like it plain. How about it?" he asked, dropping to both knees and begging like a puppy dog.

14 Christopher smiled reluctantly. "All right, sounds good." He straightened his hat and yanked Tony off the ground. "Thanks," he said, buffing Tony affectionately in the shoulder.

15 "What are friends for?" Tony called out as he ran ahead.

16 A few days later, Tony and Christopher were sitting together in the school cafeteria when they noticed a new boy at a nearby table. The boys spotted him again in the schoolyard at recess. He was sitting on the grass, leafing through a binder. Christopher and Tony jogged over to him.

17 "Hi, I'm Chris, and this is Tony," Christopher said, juggling a baseball from hand to hand.

18 "I'm Jason. My family just moved here from Austin," the boy said, squinting up at the boys who were **distracting** him from the one bright spot in his day.

19 "What have you got there? Are those baseball cards?" Christopher dropped down beside Jason.

20 "Yeah, I've been collecting them for years." Jason carefully flipped the pages, pointing out his favorites.

21 "Wow! You've got a Nolan Ryan rookie card!" Christopher exclaimed, tapping a blue-framed card on the page.

22 Jason pulled out the card and handed it to Christopher. "You can have it."

23 Christopher's mouth dropped open and his eyes grew wide. "I can't take this!"

24 "Sure you can! I've got more," Jason said, suddenly happy for the first time in many days. "Baseball is my favorite sport."

25   "Mine, too! I play on a team. How about you?"

26   "I used to play back in Austin. I want to try out for a team here at the start of next season."

27   "Maybe you could try out for my team, the Cheetahs. What do you play?"

28   "Shortstop," Jason said, closing his binder and standing up.

29   "Hey, do you want to come see our game next Saturday? My parents could give you a ride," Christopher suggested.

30   Tony frowned. "You only have room in the car for one more, Chris, and I always hitch a ride with you."

31   Christopher looked up at Tony. "Is it okay if Jason rides with me this week? You can always ask your mom to give you a ride."

32   For a moment, Tony was speechless. He stared at the two boys and the binder and felt like he was miles away. Then he said, "Sure. Whatever," and walked away.

33   For the next month, Christopher spent all of his free time with Jason. They were together almost **nonstop**. Tony stopped going to games, so Christopher only saw him at school. Christopher felt a wall going up between them. Since Tony never wanted to get together anymore, Christopher invited Jason over for pizza after the games.

Based on details on this page, what can you conclude about who is responsible for Christopher and Tony not spending time with each other anymore? Record the details and your conclusion on the **Draw Conclusions Chart.**

How would this part of the story be different if it were written from Christopher's first-person point of view?

Underline the details about how the three boys behave after Christopher races to the phone. Based on those details, what conclusion can you draw about the boys and their friendship? Add the details and your conclusion to the **Draw Conclusions Chart.**

34   "It's cool to eat pizza with someone who likes a lot of toppings. Tony eats his plain," Christopher told Jason after the last game.

35   "That's weird. And isn't his favorite sport soccer? What's wrong with that guy?" Jason said with a laugh.

36   "Nothing," Christopher said, his voice sounding harsh and **defensive**. "Lots of people love soccer."

37   "More than baseball, though? It's a good thing you don't hang out with him anymore."

38   Christopher chewed thoughtfully. All of a sudden, his pizza tasted like cardboard. He swallowed hard and stood up with a determined look on his face.

39   "Where are you going?" Jason asked nervously, knowing that he'd gone too far in bad-mouthing Tony.

40   "To call Tony," Christopher said. "Soccer season is coming up, and we're both going to need a friend who knows how to dribble! Come on!" he laughed, racing Jason to the phone.

41   As the three boys joked on the phone, Christopher felt the wall between him and Tony begin to crumble.

42   "Want to come over for pizza?" he asked Tony. "Jason can help you pick off the toppings. After all, like you always say, what are friends for?"

43   Before the pizza even had time to get cold, Tony had joined them. All three boys laughed and cheered together.

Analyze

What is the theme, or main message, of this short story?

Vocabulary: Greek and Latin Prefixes and Roots

Many English words contain word parts that come from Greek or Latin. A **root** is the main part of a word. A **prefix** is a group of letters that is added to the beginning of a root. Recognizing common roots and prefixes can help you figure out the meaning of unfamiliar words that have those word parts. For example, the word *bicycle* contains the Greek prefix *bi-*, meaning "two," and the root *cycle*, which comes from the Greek word for wheel.

Try It Read this sentence from "What Are Friends For?"

> The crowd groaned and seemed almost to **deflate**.

The word *deflate* comes from the Latin prefix *de-*, which means "the opposite" and the Latin root *flare*, which means "to blow." Based on this information, can you tell what the word *deflate* means?

▶ Discuss ▷ **Brainstorm other words that have the prefix *de-* or the root *flare*.**

The chart below includes words from the story that have Greek or Latin origins. Use the meaning of the word parts to figure out the definition of each word.

Word	Word Parts and Meanings	Definition of Word
reassuring p. 49	*re-*, "again" *assure*, "to make secure"	
distracting p. 50	*dis-*, "away" *tract*, "to pull or drag"	
nonstop p. 51	*non-*, "not" *stop*, "to end"	
defensive p. 52	*de-*, "away" *fend*, "to push"	

Respond to Text: Point of View

The stories "Things That Go Thump in the Night" and "What Are Friends For?" are told using different points of view:

"Things That Go Thump in the Night"   **first-person point of view**

"What Are Friends For?"   **third-person point of view**

Try It Think about what you learned about the characters in each story.

 Discuss **How did point of view affect your understanding of the story and how you related to the characters? Did the first-person point of view in "Things That Go Thump in the Night" help you better identify with the main character? Did the third-person point of view in "What Are Friends For?" help you better understand the thoughts, feelings, and actions of all the characters?**

On Your Own Compare and contrast the different points of view used in the stories. Describe how the point of view of each story affected your reading experience. Give examples from the texts to support your response. Use the next page to help you plan your response. Then write your paragraph on a separate sheet of paper.

Checklist for a Good Response

A good paragraph

✔ describes the point of view used in each story.

✔ includes specific examples to compare and contrast the points of view.

✔ explains how point of view affected your reading experience.

✔ includes a topic sentence, supporting ideas, and a concluding statement.

How Point of View Affected My Reading Experience

1. **Topic Sentence** Include this information in your first sentence:

   "Things That Go Thump in the Night" is written in _____

   _____ and "What Are Friends For?" is written in _____

   _____.

2. **Detail Sentences** The body of your paragraph should include sentences that tell how point of view affected your reading experience. Use this chart to organize your supporting details.

	"Things That Go Thump in the Night"	**"What Are Friends For?"**
Which character(s) do I learn the most about?		
How does my knowledge of the characters' actions, thoughts, and feelings affect my attitude toward them?		
How does the narrator shape my understanding of the story?		

3. **Concluding Sentence** Your concluding sentence should restate in a fresh way how point of view affected your reading experience.

   _____

   _____

On a separate sheet of paper, write your paragraph.

Read on Your Own

Read the story independently three times, using the skills you have learned. Then answer the Comprehension Check questions.

First Read | Practice the first-read skills you learned in this lesson.

Second Read | Practice the second-read skills you learned in this lesson.

Third Read | Think critically about the story.

The Wolf Who Cried Boy

Draw Inferences
Underline the details that the wolf gives about himself. The first one has been done for you. Think about what kind of character the wolf is.

Point of View Think about how the wolf describes the boy and how this part of the story would be different if it were told from the boy's point of view.

1   Once upon a time long ago, I enjoyed strolling through my lovely green meadow and skipping about in the sunshine. One of my favorite activities was rolling in the sweet-smelling flowers. I bothered no one, and no one bothered me. I was a happy wolf with the great big beautiful outdoors as my playground.

2   Then one day, everything changed. A boy with some sheep took over my hillside meadow and ruined my beautiful, peaceful life!

3   I could hear him coming from the other side of the hill. "What's that terrible noise?" I asked myself. It sounded like whistling. And the whistling was followed by the bleating of what sounded like an entire army of sheep! Then I heard the boy call out, "Lots of grass for you here!" I quickly ran behind a large tree, unsure of what problem was headed my way. When he reached the top of the hill, I saw what I can only describe as a very mean looking boy holding a sturdy walking stick.

4   "He can be up to no good at all," I said to myself. "Why, I'm sure that he could beat me quite soundly with that stick! And once I'm down, I feel certain that he would command those sheep to **trample** me into the ground!"

5   I did what I had to do. I ran out from behind the tree and called for help. "Help! Help! There's a boy with sheep here in my meadow! Someone, please come quick!" I began to jump up and down and wave my arms back and forth.

6   At that moment, the boy began to scream, crying even louder than I. "WOLF! WOLF! COME PROTECT THE SHEEP! HELP!" He shook his walking stick at me and, of course, I ran down the hillside as fast as lightning to get away from him.

7   Soon, the townspeople came running. I don't know what happened when they reached the boy. I stayed in my hiding place for the rest of the day and night.

8   The next morning, I hoped the boy and his sheep would be gone, but just my luck, they were still there. I decided I would try to talk to him. Maybe I could **explain** that this was my meadow. But when I tried to approach him, he began screaming again, so I ran away.

9   From my hiding place, I saw the people from the village come running again to find out what was wrong. On their way back to the village, they looked quite angry for some reason.

Idioms, Adages, and Proverbs Think about the meaning of the expression "as fast as lightning."

Critical Thinking Think about whether the wolf understands why the boy acts the way he does.

Draw Conclusions

Underline details about the boy. What conclusion can you draw about why he runs away at the end?

Critical Thinking

Think about the theme, or main message, of this story.

10   Finally, on the third day, I decided that I would no longer put up with such behavior from the boy. I was sure that we could work something out. Maybe the boy didn't know that the lovely green meadow with its green grass and fragrant flowers belonged to me. I decided to talk to him face to face. I would not beat around the bush. I would simply tell him that the meadow was mine.

11   But just as before, as soon as I stepped out from behind the tree, the boy began screaming, "WOLF! WOLF! COME PROTECT THE SHEEP! HELP!"

12   This time I decided not to run away. I would stand my ground and ask the townspeople to help me talk to the unreasonable boy. I stood impatiently, tapping my foot and waiting. But no one came. The boy continued to yell. Still, no one came.

13   The boy grew hoarse and only then did he stop screaming. He looked at me and raised his stick. I looked back and gave him my biggest, toothiest grin, hoping at last to win him over. Instead, he turned pale and ran away from me, back up the hill toward town.

14   The sheep looked up briefly and then continued munching away on the grass. I breathed a deep sigh of relief and settled back down for a roll across my wonderful meadow. We never saw that troublesome boy again, so the sheep and I learned to share the meadow peacefully.

✅ Comprehension Check

1. The wolf says that the people "looked quite angry for some reason." Why were the people angry? Use details from the text to draw an inference.

_____

_____

_____

_____

2. From what point of view is this story told? How did you determine the point of view?

_____

_____

_____

_____

3. What conclusion can you draw about why the boy runs away at the end?

_____

_____

_____

_____

4. What does the wolf mean when he says, "I would not beat around the bush"?

_____

_____

_____

5. Read this sentence from the story.

Maybe I could explain that this was my meadow.

The word _explain_ contains the Latin prefix _ex-_, which means "out," and the root word _plain_, which comes from a Latin word that means "smooth" or "clear." Based on this information, write what the word _explain_ means.

_____

_____

_____

6. Read this sentence from the story.

And once I'm down, I feel certain that he would command those sheep to trample me into the ground.

Underline the words that help you understand the meaning of _trample_. What does the word _trample_ mean?

_____

_____

_____

Lesson 3
Drama

A drama, or play, is a story that is written to be performed by actors on a stage. A drama includes story elements, such as characters, setting, and plot. However, a drama is different from a story or a novel in several ways. First, a drama is divided into acts and scenes, not chapters. Also, a drama is made up of lines of dialogue for each character, instead of paragraphs of dialogue and description, as you would read in a story. The plot of a play unfolds through the dialogue. The writer of a play does not have to describe the settings in too much detail. That's because the scenery and props on the stage bring the settings to life. Look at this photo. What do you think is happening in this play?

Skills Focus

The Case of the Missing Ring

| Make Predictions | Elements of Drama |

The Money Goes Missing

| Summarize | Character Motivation |

Practice the Skill

When you make a **prediction**, you use what you know to make a good guess about what will happen in the future. As you read a story or a drama, you use what you have read so far to predict what event will take place next or what a character will decide to do. You can read some of the story and predict what might happen to the characters or what events might occur next. You can read most of the story and make a prediction about how it might end.

A prediction should always be based on evidence from the text. Sometimes, you may need to revise, or change, your prediction as you read more of a story or a drama.

Try It Read these lines from a drama.

> NARRATOR: The house was dark and deserted. The two boys silently approached the steps, wondering if they should open the door and walk in or wait for the others. They heard a noise coming from inside the house and looked at each other.

Discuss **Think about what a dark and deserted house might look like. What does the phrase "dark and deserted" make you think of? Ask yourself how you would feel if you stood outside such a house, making your way up the steps. Use this information to make a prediction about what the boys might do next.**

As you read, complete the Make Predictions Chart on page 233.

Practice the Skill

Second Read **Elements of Drama**

All dramas contain some common elements. A drama is divided into large sections called **acts** and smaller ones called **scenes**. The **setting** describes the location and time in which the events take place. Every time the setting changes, a new scene starts. The **cast of characters** at the beginning of the play lists all the characters who will appear, in order, and gives a brief description of each one. **Dialogue** is the words that the characters speak. Near some lines of dialogue, you may see italicized words enclosed in parentheses, such as "(*sadly*)." These words, called **stage directions**, tell the actors how to move or speak.

Try It Read this short scene from a drama.

SYLVIA: (*looks scared*) Why are you following me?

JERRY: (*whispering*) I'm trying to warn you. Someone is after you.

SYLVIA: (*laughing*) That's ridiculous. I haven't done anything wrong.

JERRY: (*looking around*) That's not what they think.

SYLVIA: (*angrily*) Who is "they"?

> **Discuss** **Who are the characters? Underline their names. What is Sylvia supposed to do in her second line of dialogue? Circle the stage direction. How is Jerry supposed to speak in his first piece of dialogue? Circle the stage direction.**

As you read, record your answers to questions about the elements of drama on the Close Reading Worksheet on page 234. ✏➡

Purpose for Reading
Read along with your teacher. Each time, read for a different purpose.

First Read Focus on making predictions.

Second Read Focus on the elements of the drama.

Third Read Focus on evaluating the drama critically.

The Case of the Missing Ring

Based on the cast of characters, who do you predict might be involved with the missing ring? Write your prediction and a clue on the **Make Predictions Chart**.

What is Constance's relationship to Barnaby? How do you know? Circle text that tells you.

What do you think are important details of the setting? Why?

CAST OF CHARACTERS

CONSTANCE, Mrs. Butterfield's neighbor

BARNABY, Constance's friend

MRS. BUTTERFIELD, the lady of the house

HOLLY FISHER, a detective

CECILY, Mrs. Butterfield's daughter

Act 1

Scene 1

SETTING: *England, 1942. Lights up on a large, grandly decorated living room. Half-full glasses and plates of half-eaten cake are scattered around the room.*

(*Constance cracks open a large door that leads to the rest of the house. She peeks inside, sees nobody is in the room, and opens the door. She waves in Barnaby and quietly closes the door behind them.*)

1 BARNABY: So where is the diamond you were so excited about?

2 CONSTANCE: It's not just *any* diamond, Barnaby. It's *the* Butterfield family jewel. That ring is worth millions!

(*Mrs. Butterfield is heard sobbing.*)

3 BARNABY: Well, where is it?

4 CONSTANCE: Shh! Quiet! They're coming. Look useful. Help me clean up this mess.

(*Constance and Barnaby stack the plates of half-eaten cake. Mrs. Butterfield, Cecily, and Holly enter.*)

5 MRS. BUTTERFIELD: (*sobbing*) I believe the last people to leave were Mr. and Mrs. Cornwall, but certainly they—

6 HOLLY: I'm sorry, Mrs. Butterfield. (*to Constance and Barnaby*) Excuse me—

Whom will Holly question Mrs. Butterfield about next? Write your prediction and the clue you used to make it on the **Make Predictions Chart**.

Circle the stage directions that help you understand that Mrs. Butterfield is upset.

How do the stage directions help you understand Holly's first line of dialogue in paragraph 9? Circle the clues.

How might the white footprint help Holly solve the mystery of the missing ring? Support your answer with evidence from the text.

7   CECILY: Oh my! Constance! Ms. Fisher has asked that this room be left untouched. There might be evidence, dear.

(*Constance and Barnaby glance at each other and stop stacking plates. Holly watches them closely.*)

8   MRS. BUTTERFIELD: (*continuing*) Certainly the Cornwalls aren't **suspects** in the crime, are they?

9   HOLLY: I'm afraid everyone is a suspect, Mrs. Butterfield. (*to Constance*) Constance, is it? (*Constance smiles and nods.*) May I speak with the Butterfields alone, please?

10 CONSTANCE: Of course! Cecily, dear, I'll just be outside.

(*Constance and Barnaby exit.*)

11 HOLLY: Mrs. Butterfield, how long has your family known Constance?

12 MRS. BUTTERFIELD: Why, Constance and Cecily were friends before they could speak. Constance is like family.

13 CECILY: Yes, you don't have to worry about—

14 HOLLY: She was at the house, so we need to consider—

15 MRS. BUTTERFIELD: Absolutely not! I won't hear another word. Constance is to be left out of this. Do you understand? Come, Cecily, I need to retire.

(*Mrs. Butterfield and Cecily exit. Holly lingers. She notices a footprint of white dust. She wipes the dust with a finger, inspects it, and exits, engaged in thought.*)

Scene 2

SETTING: *Constance and Barnaby are whispering excitedly in a garden outside the house.*

16 BARNABY: So, where is it?

17 CONSTANCE: Last night, I was helping Mrs. Butterfield into bed and noticed she had left the ring on the dresser.

18 BARNABY: But where is it now?

19 CONSTANCE: She drifted off to sleep, complaining about how Mr. Butterfield won't buy her some silly horse and how she was going to get even with him somehow.

20 BARNABY: Yes, yes, but where is the ring?

21 CONSTANCE: Well, I had to hide it because I promised Cecily I'd stay the night. But I hid it! I hid the ring!

22 BARNABY: And where did you hide it?

23 CONSTANCE: (*laughing*) The flour! I hid it in the flour!

Act 2
Scene 1

SETTING: *Several hours later in the living room. Holly has been questioning Mrs. Butterfield for a while.*

24 MRS. BUTTERFIELD: I don't see what the horse has to do with anything. That's really not a concern any longer.

(*Cecily enters.*)

What, if anything, do you think the horse has to do with the missing ring? Write your prediction and two clues on the **Make Predictions Chart**.

Why does a new act begin on this page? Circle the text that supports your answer.

What is similar about how Mrs. Butterfield responds to questioning about the horse and how she responds to questioning about Constance at the end of act 1, scene 1?

Check your predictions. Write what actually happens on the **Make Predictions Chart**. Write a ✓ if your prediction was correct and an ✗ if it was wrong.

Does Cecily know what has happened? Support your answer with evidence from the text. ✏️⊐

Analyze

Does Mrs. Butterfield act like a guilty person earlier in the play? How? ✏️⊐

25 CECILY: Pardon me, Ms. Fisher. Mother, the cook said to tell you he **disposed** of the flour, so there will be no cake today.

26 MRS. BUTTERFIELD: (*vexed*) HE DID WHAT? WHY?

27 CECILY: Mother! I admit it will be hard, but you'll have to **manage** without cake for a day. Rats got into the flour last night.

28 MRS. BUTTERFIELD: But that flour was worth . . . worth . . .

29 HOLLY: (*figuring it out*) Worth what, Mrs. Butterfield?

30 MRS. BUTTERFIELD: (*sobbing*) MILLIONS!

31 HOLLY: Cecily, I suggest you find Constance and her friend. We are about to hear a very interesting story.

(*Cecily exits in shock.*)

32 MRS. BUTTERFIELD: Constance stole the ring! I saw her.

33 HOLLY: But you realized it was the perfect plot, didn't you? You could sell the ring to buy your horse, and no one would know. You followed Constance and saw her hide it in the flour, and you were going to go back for it when I left today. Let's hope the police find that as interesting as I do, ma'am. Let's go.

(*Holly leads a sobbing Mrs. Butterfield offstage.*)

END OF PLAY

Vocabulary: Multiple-Meaning Words

Many words have more than one meaning. For example, the word *fly* can mean "a small insect with wings." *Fly* can also mean "to soar in the air." These are called **multiple-meaning words**. To understand which meaning of a word an author intended, look at the context. Think about the different meanings of the word. Ask yourself which meaning makes the most sense.

Try It Read the word below and its meanings. Then read the sentence, and choose the meaning that best fits in the sentence.

> **present:** a gift OR the time happening now
>
> Grandma got me a new skateboard as a present.

If you don't know which meaning of *present* fits best, ask yourself if a new skateboard could be a gift or is something that is happening now.

▶ Discuss ▶ **Choose the correct meaning of *present*.**

The following words appear in "The Case of the Missing Ring." Read the sentence in which the word appears, and circle the correct meaning.

1. **suspects,** p. 66: …Certainly the Cornwalls aren't suspects in the crime…
   a. people accused of a crime   b. to believe something

2. **manage,** p. 68: …you'll have to manage without cake for a day.
   a. take care of   b. get by

3. **disposed,** p. 68: …he disposed of the flour, so there will be no cake today.
   a. threw out   b. preferring or tending toward something

Practice the Skill

When you tell a friend about a great movie you saw, you do not include every single detail about it. Instead, you **summarize** the story in your own words. A summary is a short description of a longer work. When you summarize, you include only the main ideas and most important details of a text. You can summarize a whole text, a page of a text, or just a paragraph. If you can summarize a story or a drama, it shows that you understand what the story or drama is about.

Try It Read this paragraph from a student's book report.

Harriet, the twelve-year-old main character, wants to be a star basketball player on her high school basketball team. The team is called the Tigers, and they are 3–0 this season so far. Harriet works hard every day at practice, which is from four to six in the afternoon. Eventually, her hard work pays off, and she receives the Best Player of the Year award.

> Discuss **How would you summarize this paragraph about Harriet? What are the most important things about her? Circle those things. Now reread the paragraph, and cross out the details that are not necessary to include in a summary.**

As you read, record your answers to questions about summarizing on the Close Reading Worksheet on page 235.

Practice the Skill

Motivation is the reason why a character acts, thinks, and feels the way that he or she does. When you are trying to determine a character's motivation, you need to think about what makes that character say a certain thing, behave in a certain way, or feel a certain emotion. The motivations of a character can change as events happen and the character changes and grows. Understanding a character's motivations will help you better understand a story or drama.

Try It Read this paragraph.

> The young girl at the athletic club looked out the window. She thought about how far she had come. She had worked tirelessly at the gym to get in the best shape she could. She would show those trainers. No one would ever laugh at her again.

Discuss Think about what the girl is feeling. What might have happened in her life to make her feel this way? Which words in the text are clues to her motivation? Underline them.

As you read, complete the Character Motivation Chart on page 236.

The Money Goes Missing

What is the most important idea in the opening scene of the play?

Why does Kalisha make the announcement at the assembly? Underline clues in her dialogue and then complete row 1 of the **Character Motivation Chart**.

CAST OF CHARACTERS

KALISHA, student council president

GEORGE, student council vice president

TITO, student council secretary

MAI-LIN, student council treasurer

Act 1
Scene 1

SETTING: *Lights and sounds suggest a crowded student **assembly** at a present-day middle school. The student council officers, Kalisha, George, Tito, and Mai-Lin, enter. Kalisha goes to the podium and addresses the crowd.*

1   KALISHA: Hey, everyone! Let's hear it for your student council officers, who have some exciting news to share! (*loud cheers*) We are here to announce that we raised over two hundred dollars at the wrapping-paper sale last week! (*cheers*) That means next fall, when you are eating lunch, you'll be looking at a mural designed by our very own Tito Juarez! (*cheers*) Tell them, Tito!

(*The crowd cheers loudly as Tito steps to the microphone. George tries to hand Tito a metal box. Tito is dazzled by the audience and doesn't notice. Mai-Lin grabs the box from George. They have a quiet but heated conversation during Tito's speech.*)

Summarize what happens in scene 1.

2   TITO: Thanks, everyone! I'm thrilled that we raised enough money for the supplies we need to put a mural in the cafeteria, and I am honored that it was my design that was chosen. (*The audience cheers.*) One of the council's goals is to make Hopper Middle School a more pleasant place to be every day, and that's what this project is all about!

At what point does Mai-Lin first become annoyed? Use evidence from the text to support your answer.

(*Sounds of cheers as the student council officers wave and move from the podium.*)

Scene 2

SETTING: *As the crowd sounds fade, the lights shift, and the student council officers move into a classroom.*

3   TITO: That was awesome, standing up there while the crowd went wild with **admiration**! Wasn't that fantastic?

4   MAI-LIN: (*annoyed*) I don't know. I was too busy worrying that we'd lose all the money we raised.

The Money Goes Missing   **73**

What is an important detail that you would include in a summary of this page?

Why is Mai-Lin angrier at George than anyone else is? Support your answer with evidence from the text. Complete row 2 of the **Character Motivation Chart.**

Which character seems to act most like a leader? Use evidence from the text to support your answer.

5   TITO: (*in his own world*) They loved us!

6   GEORGE: Oh, please. The money was safe. I was holding it the whole time. Well, I was until you ripped it away.

7   KALISHA: What's going on here?

8   MAI-LIN: George brought the money to the assembly!

(*Everyone looks at George.*)

9   GEORGE: What? What's wrong with that?

10   MAI-LIN: What's wrong with that is I'm responsible for the money, and we agreed to leave it in Mr. Hart's desk.

11   GEORGE: I just thought it would be like a trophy that we could hold up and use to get the crowd excited.

12   TITO: Yeah, they were really impressed! Wasn't it great?

(*Mai-Lin rolls her eyes.*)

13   KALISHA: OK, everyone, settle down. Let's not get paranoid. Mai-Lin is right, George. The money should have stayed in the room. But, luckily, nothing happened, so let's drop it, OK?

(*After a tense moment, Mai-Lin and George grumble "fine," and the student council members sit to begin their meeting.*)

14 KALISHA: OK. So, speaking of the money, the first order of business is to give Tito some money to buy the first round of supplies.

15 TITO: Cool! I'll go to the art supply store right after school.

(*Mai-Lin opens the cash box, and her jaw drops.*)

16 MAI-LIN: I knew it! The money is gone! (*glaring at George*) You'd better have a good explanation.

(*Everyone gasps. George throws up his hands. Kalisha looks in the box. Tito's good mood turns to gloominess.*)

Which character's motivation is to clear his or her name? Support your answer with evidence from the text. Complete row 3 of the **Character Motivation Chart**.

Act 2
Scene 1

SETTING: *The student council members are still in the classroom. They have been there for a while, trying to solve the mystery. Tito's head is on the desk. George is pacing. Kalisha is deep in thought. Mai-Lin's arms are crossed.*

17 TITO: I was so excited to paint that mural.

18 GEORGE: The money was in the box, I promise. I looked!

19 MAI-LIN: Just to **clarify**, did you happen to look in your wallet, too?

20 GEORGE: Mai-Lin, I didn't steal the money! It's just—

21 MAI-LIN: (*interrupting George*) stolen!

22 GEORGE: (*at the same time as Mai-Lin*) missing.

23 KALISHA: Enough, you guys! George, tell me everything you did before the assembly. Let's retrace your steps.

24 GEORGE: OK. I got to school late this morning, so everyone had already left for the assembly. I took the money out of Mr. Hart's desk and started toward the **auditorium**. Mr. Hart stopped me and reminded me to sign in at the office since I was late. So I ran to the office and then went straight to the assembly. It was in my hands the whole time!

Why does Kalisha run offstage? Support your answer with evidence from the text. Complete row 4 of the **Character Motivation Chart**.

Who is the best problem solver on the student council? Support your answer with evidence from the text.

Compare and Contrast

Compare and contrast Mai-Lin's and Kalisha's responses to the missing money. How are they the same? How are they different? Support your answer with evidence from the text.

(*Mai-Lin rolls her eyes. Kalisha thinks for a moment.*)

25 KALISHA: (*brightly*) You went to the office on your way?

26 GEORGE: Yeah. Mr. Hart told me to.

(*Kalisha runs offstage. Everyone else is confused. She runs back in carrying an identical box.*)

27 KALISHA: I found it! You had to put down the box to sign in, right? You must have picked up the wrong box!

(*Mai-Lin and George are relieved. Tito is happy.*)

28 TITO: I think I'll go and buy those supplies right now, before anything else happens. We've had enough excitement for one day.

END OF PLAY

Vocabulary: Greek and Latin Suffixes and Roots

Many English words contain word parts that come from Greek or Latin. A **root** is the main part of a word. A **suffix** is a group of letters that is added to the end of a root. Recognizing common roots and suffixes can help you figure out the meaning of unfamiliar words that have those word parts. For example, the word *flexible* comes from the Latin root *flec*, meaning "bend," and the Latin suffix *-ible*, meaning "able to."

Try It Read this sentence from "The Money Goes Missing."

*Lights and sounds suggest a crowded student **assembly** at a present-day middle school.*

The word *assembly* comes from the Latin root *simul*, which means "together," and the Greek suffix *-y*, which forms a noun.

> Discuss > **Brainstorm what *assembly* means.**

The chart below includes words from the story that have Greek or Latin origins. Use the meaning of the word parts to figure out the definition of each word.

Word	Word Parts and Meanings	Definition of Word
admiration p. 73	root *admir*, "to wonder at" suffix *-ation*, forms nouns from verbs	
auditorium p. 75	root *aud*, "to hear or listen" suffix *-orium*, "place for"	
clarify p. 75	root *clar*, "clear" suffix *-ify*, "to make or cause to become"	

Respond to Text: Elements of Drama

"The Money Goes Missing" is a drama. Dramas tell a story but in a distinct format.

Try It Think about what you have just learned about dramas.

 Discuss ⟩ **How does the structure (acts and scenes) help you follow the events? How do the stage directions and dialogue reveal what the characters are like?**

On Your Own Write about what makes drama a distinct form of writing. Think about the structure of "The Money Goes Missing." In your writing, include a description of the role that each element in the drama plays. Use the next page to help you plan your response. Then write your paragraph(s) on a separate sheet of paper.

Checklist for a Good Response

A good paragraph

✔ shows your understanding of why dramas are written.

✔ shows your understanding of what a drama is.

✔ includes the elements contained in a drama.

✔ describes each of the elements.

✔ includes a topic sentence, supporting ideas, and a concluding statement.

✔ has complete sentences.

✔ is free of spelling and grammatical errors.

My Description of How Drama Is Distinct

1. **Topic Sentence** Include this information as your topic sentence:

   Based on what I just learned, drama is a distinct type of writing

   because _____ .

2. **Detail Sentences** The sentences of your paragraph should provide details about how the elements of drama were used in "The Money Goes Missing."

Element	Details
acts	
scenes	
setting	
stage directions	

3. **Concluding Sentence** Your final sentence should restate what you have learned about drama with a new twist.

   _____

   _____

On a separate sheet of paper, write your paragraph.

Read on Your Own

Read the drama independently three times, using the skills you have learned. Then answer the Comprehension Check questions.

First Read	Practice the first-read skills you learned in this lesson.
Second Read	Practice the second-read skills you learned in this lesson.
Third Read	Think critically about the drama.

Eloisa's Best Friend

Summarize Underline important details that you would include in a summary of the setting of this drama. One detail has been underlined for you.

Elements of Drama How do you know Legato is not a human character? Circle the text that tells you this.

CAST OF CHARACTERS

ELOISA, a fourth-grade girl

LEGATO, her talking cat

MR. FLOREZ, Eloisa's grandfather

ALEJANDRO, her best friend

MRS. PEÑA, Alejandro's mother

Act 1
Scene 1

SETTING: _Eloisa and Mr. Florez's home._ _Lights up on Eloisa and Legato in the front yard, wrestling in a friendly and playful way._

1 ELOISA: (_laughing_) OK! I'll give you the treats! I promise! Just stop tickling me!

(_Legato stops tickling Eloisa, and she catches her breath._)

2   LEGATO: (*begging like a dog*) I beg of you, Señorita. Release the treats! Arf!

3   ELOISA: (*laughing again and running away*) Never!

4   LEGATO: Hey! I lowered myself to begging like a dog!

(*Legato runs after Eloisa offstage. Mr. Florez, Mrs. Peña, and Alejandro enter.*)

5   MR. FLOREZ: Eloisa! (*no answer*) Eloisa! (*still no answer*) I'm sorry, Alejandro. She was just out here playing with Legato. I'm sure they'll be back soon.

6   MRS. PEÑA: I'm afraid we won't be able to wait.

7   ALEJANDRO: But, Mama! I can't leave without telling Eloisa good-bye. She doesn't even know I'm leaving.

8   MRS. PEÑA: That is how life works out sometimes, son. Perhaps we can visit next summer and you can see her then.

9   ALEJANDRO: What? We will only be a few hours away!

10   MRS. PEÑA: Not now, Alejandro. (*turning to Mr. Florez*) Thank you for having us without any notice, Mr. Florez. Please tell Eloisa we stopped by and that we will try to visit soon.

(*Mrs. Peña and Mr. Florez exit. Alejandro lingers until his mother calls from offstage. He exits.*)

Make Predictions
Think about how Eloisa will feel when she finds out that she missed saying good-bye to her best friend before he moved away.

Character Motivation Put a box around one thing Alejandro says and one thing he does that show you his strong desire to say good-bye to Eloisa.

Critical Thinking
Think about which character in this drama is the funniest and which one is the most serious. Support your judgments with evidence from the text.

Scene 2

SETTING: *Lights fade up on the Florez's front porch. Eloisa sits on the porch, crying. Her grandfather and Legato are hugging and consoling her. Lights fade out.*

Act 2
Scene 1

SETTING: *The Florez's home. Eloisa is standing in the front yard, looking around unenthusiastically.*

11 ELOISA: (*flatly*) Come out, come out, wherever you are. (*rolls her eyes*) I don't know! I give up!

(*Legato peeks out from behind a tree.*)

12 LEGATO: Excuse me? Unless my razor-sharp hearing fools me, I think I heard "give up" come out of your mouth.

13 ELOISA: Your hearing is perfect. I don't want to play.

14 LEGATO: (*coming out*) No problem. That tree was giving me a rash anyway. Do you want to jump rope?

15 ELOISA: No.

16 LEGATO: Shoot marbles? Throw jacks? Chase our tails?

17 ELOISA: (*sharply*) No, Legato! I don't want to play. Period!

18 LEGATO: Oh. (*hurt*) You know, Alejandro wasn't your only friend. I'm your friend, too.

Summarize
Think about two main ideas and two details you would include in a summary of act 2, scene 1.

Character Motivation
Think about each character's motivation in act 1, scene 2. Think about why Mr. Florez and Legato are hugging Eloisa. Think about why Eloisa is crying.

Elements of Drama
Which stage directions give you clues about how Eloisa says her lines on this page? Circle the clues in the text.

19 ELOISA: Yeah, but you're just a cat, Legato. Go away.

(*Legato goes to hug Eloisa, but she shrugs him off.*)

20 ELOISA: I'm serious. Leave me alone!

(*Legato walks offstage dragging his tail. Lights fade out.*)

Scene 2

SETTING: *Later the same day. The sun is setting. Eloisa is on the porch calling Legato anxiously.*

21 ELOISA: Legato! (*no response*) Legato! Here, kitty!

(*Eloisa starts to cry. Mr. Florez enters from the house.*)

22 MR. FLOREZ: Come inside and get ready for bed, Eloisa. He'll be home in the morning, sitting on the porch hungry.

23 ELOISA: (*crying*) I was so mean to him, Grandpa. I told him to leave me alone. Please let me wait up for him!

24 MR. FLOREZ: (*considering*) OK. I'll wait, too.

(*Lights fade out as they call for Legato.*)

Make Predictions
Where do you think Legato is in act 2, scene 2? Think about your prediction.

Critical Thinking
Think about how Eloisa and Legato interact differently in act 2, scene 1 than they do in act 1, scene 1.

Scene 3

Summarize Put an X over a detail that you would not include in a summary of the last scene of the play.

Elements of Drama Think about why a new scene begins at this point in the story.

Critical Thinking Think about whether the title of this drama, "Eloisa's Best Friend," applies to Alejandro or Legato. Support your answer with evidence from the text.

SETTING: *The lights come up, and it is the next morning. Eloisa and her grandfather are asleep on the porch. Alejandro runs onto the stage.*

25   ALEJANDRO: Eloisa! Eloisa!

26   ELOISA: (*waking, surprised*) Alejandro! What are you—

27   ALEJANDRO: (*interrupting and giving her a big hug*) I've come back to give you a hug, and tell you I miss you, and say a proper good-bye!

28   ELOISA: I miss you, too! But how did you get here?

29   ALEJANDRO: Legato convinced my mom to drive me here in the middle of the night. He should be a lawyer!

30   ELOISA: (*confused*) Legato?

(*Legato and Mrs. Peña enter. Mr. Florez wakes up. Eloisa stands with her jaw dropped.*)

31   LEGATO: What's the matter? Cat got your tongue?

(*Eloisa laughs as she runs to hug Legato.*)

END OF PLAY

✔ Comprehension Check

1. Write a summary of this drama in one or two sentences.

_____

_____

_____

2. Read these lines of dialogue from the drama.

   **ELOISA: (_flatly_) Come out, come out, wherever you are.
   (_rolls her eyes_) I don't know! I give up!**

   The word _roll_ has many meanings. Write the meaning of the word
   roll as it is used here. Then, write another meaning of the word _roll_
   and use it in a sentence.

   _____

   _____

   _____

3. What is Legato's motivation for going to get Alejandro?

   _____

   _____

   _____

4. Act 1, scene 2 of this drama is very short and does not contain dialogue. How do you understand what happens without dialogue?

_____

_____

_____

5. What do you predict Eloisa will say to Legato at the end of the drama?

_____

_____

_____

6. Read these lines of dialogue from the drama.

> **ALEJANDRO: (*interrupting and giving her a big hug*) I've come back to give you a hug, and tell you I miss you, and say a proper good-bye!**

The word *interrupting* has a root and a suffix. The Latin root *rup* means "to burst." The suffix *-ing* makes the verb present tense. Write a definition of the word *interrupting*, and use it in a new sentence.

_____

_____

_____

Lesson 4
Poetry

In a **poem**, a poet uses carefully chosen words to express ideas and feelings or to tell a story. Rhyme, rhythm, and colorful descriptions combine to create pictures with words. Poets write about everyday things in surprising ways, using vivid words to help readers gain a richer appreciation of the world around them. Look at this photo. What words might a poet use to describe the power of a waterfall?

Skills Focus

The Wind and the Moon

| Visualize | Elements of Poetry |

The Wind Tapped Like a Tired Man / Winter

| Determine the Theme | Figurative Language |

Practice the Skill

First Read **Visualize**

To **visualize** is to see something in your mind. You create a mental picture that only you can see. You use the details in a text, along with what you already know, to imagine your picture. You should also use any accompanying illustrations to help you imagine the things you are reading about. When you listen to or read poetry, pay close attention to the words, and use them to visualize the many colorful and powerful pictures that the words describe. It helps to close your eyes and try to picture what the words are saying. By doing this, you will enjoy the poem even more.

Try It Read these lines from the poem "September" by Helen Hunt Jackson.

> The golden-rod is yellow;
> The corn is turning brown;
> The trees in apple orchards
> With fruit are bending down.

Discuss **What pictures do you visualize when you hear the words of the poem? What season is it in September? What happens to many flowers, vegetables, trees, and fruits in the month of September? Put a box around the words that help you visualize. Think about what you know and what the poem says. What do you see in your mind?**

As you read, complete the Visualize Chart on page 237.

Practice the Skill

Poems are made up of different elements, or parts. Poetry is written in **verse**, or short lines. A group of lines organized within a poem is called a **stanza**. Stanzas are usually separated by a blank line space.

Poets use sound in special ways to express their ideas. **Rhyme** is the repetition of sounds at the ends of lines. Like a song, a poem has a rhythm, or beat. **Rhythm** is created by the stressed and unstressed syllables in the poem. When you stress a syllable, you say it more strongly: "MIRR-or, MIRR-or, ON the WALL." The pattern of strong and weak stresses gives the poem its **meter**.

Try It Read these lines from the poem "A Garden" by Helen Beatrix Carter.

> We have a little garden,
>   A garden of our own,
> And every day we water there
>   The seeds that we have sown.
>
> We love our little garden,
>   And tend it with such care,
> You will not find a faded leaf
>   Or blighted blossom there.

Discuss **What is the poem about? Circle the word that tells you. How many stanzas are in the poem? Number them. Which words rhyme? Underline them. Listen to the rhythm of the poem. Tap out the beats on your desk as you read the verses.**

As you read, record your answers to questions about the elements of poetry on the Close Reading Worksheet on page 238.

The Wind and the Moon

by George Macdonald

In the first stanza, ⓒircle the words that rhyme with *out*. Then underline the words that rhyme with *stare*. What is the rhyming pattern of this stanza?

Why is the wind upset with the moon?

1   Said the Wind to the Moon, "I will blow you out;
    You stare
    In the air
    Like a ghost in a chair,
5   Always looking what I am about —
    I hate to be watched; I'll blow you out."

    The Wind blew hard, and out went the Moon.
    So, deep
    On a heap
10 Of clouds to sleep,
    Down lay the Wind, and **slumbered** soon,
    Muttering low, "I've done for that Moon."

He turned in his bed; she was there again!
On high
15 In the sky,
With her one ghost eye,
The Moon shone white and alive and plain.
Said the Wind, "I will blow you out again."

The Wind blew hard, and the Moon grew dim.
20 "With my sledge,[1]
And my wedge,
I have knocked off her edge!
If only I blow right fierce and **grim**,
The creature will soon be dimmer than dim."

[1]**sledge** a large, heavy hammer

Read the second stanza on this page. How has the moon changed? Draw or describe what you see on the **Visualize Chart**.

Read the first stanza on this page aloud. Put a box around the lines that are long. Double underline the lines that are short.

What does the wind mean in the second stanza when he says he has knocked off the moon's edge?

How does the rhyme relate to the rhythm in this poem? ✎⟫

25 He blew and he blew, and she thinned to a thread.
"One puff
More's enough
To blow her to snuff!
One good puff more where the last was bred,
30 And glimmer, glimmer, glum will go the thread."

He blew a great blast, and the thread was gone.
In the air
Nowhere
Was a moonbeam bare;
35 Far off and harmless the shy stars shone —
Sure and certain the Moon was gone!

The Wind he took to his revels[2] once more;
On down,
In town,
40 Like a merry-mad clown,
He leaped and halloed with whistle and roar —
"What's that?" The glimmering thread once more!

He flew in a rage — he danced and blew;
But in vain
45 Was the pain
Of his bursting brain;
For still the broader the Moon-scrap[3] grew,
The **broader** he swelled his big cheeks and blew.

[2] **revels** merrymaking, festivities
[3] **scrap** small piece of a whole

Read the first stanza on this page. What is the wind doing? Draw or describe what you see on the **Visualize Chart.**

How is the rhythm of the poem like the wind?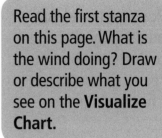

In which season of the year do you think this poem takes place? Use evidence from the text to support your answer.

The Wind and the Moon 93

Read the first stanza on this page. Draw or describe what you see on the **Visualize Chart**.

Construct

Do you think the wind could ever really make the moon disappear? What does the last stanza tell you about the moon? What else do you learn about the moon in this poem?

Slowly she grew — till she filled the night,
50 And shone
On her throne
In the sky alone,
A matchless, wonderful silvery light,
Radiant and lovely, the queen of the night.

55 Said the Wind: "What a marvel of power am I!
With my breath,
Good faith!
I blew her to death —
First blew her away right out of the sky —
60 Then blew her in; what strength have I!"

But the Moon she knew nothing about the affair;
For high
In the sky,
With her one white eye,
65 Motionless, miles above the air,
She had never heard the great Wind blare.

Vocabulary: Synonyms

Synonyms are words with similar meanings. For example, *huge* and *large* are synonyms for *big*. Notice that these words do not mean exactly the same thing. *Huge* means something is bigger than *large* or *big*. You can use synonyms to define words you do not know. In a poem, you might find synonyms right in the same stanza.

Try It Read these verses from "The Wind and the Moon."

> So, deep
> On a heap
> Of clouds to sleep,
> Down lay the Wind, and **slumbered** soon,

If you do not know what the word *slumbered* means, read the other words in the stanza. Find the synonym for *slumber*.

Discuss **Brainstorm definitions of the word *slumbered*.**

Find the words below in "The Wind and the Moon." Underline the synonyms that help you understand what each word means. Write a definition of each word, and use the word in a sentence.

1. **grim,** p. 91 _____

_____

2. **broader,** p. 93 _____

_____

3. **radiant,** p. 94 _____

_____

Practice the Skill

Determine the Theme

The **theme** of a poem is the message the poet is telling the reader. A theme is expressed in a sentence, such as "love is blind." For example, the theme of the poem "The Wind and the Moon" might be "accept those things you cannot change." To figure out the theme of a poem, first read the whole poem. Then ask yourself, "What message is the poet trying to tell me?"

Try It Read the beginning of the poem "The Fisherman" by Abbie Farwell Brown.

> The fisherman goes out at dawn
> When every one's abed,
> And from the bottom of the sea
> Draws up his daily bread.
>
> His life is strange; half on the shore
> And half upon the sea —
> Not quite a fish, and yet not quite
> The same as you and me.
>
> The fisherman has curious eyes;
> They make you feel so queer,
> As if they had seen many things
> Of wonder and of fear.

> **Discuss** Think about the theme of these stanzas. What is the fisherman like? How is he different from other people? Underline the words about the fisherman. What does the poet want to tell you about the fisherman?

As you read, record your answers to questions about theme on the Close Reading Worksheet on page 239.

Practice the Skill

Second Read | **Figurative Language**

Poets often use words to express something different from what the words usually mean. This special use of language is called **figurative language**. Poets use figurative language to create powerful images in their poems.

Some figurative language makes comparisons between two things that are really not alike. This helps you think of them in a new way. For example, a poet might write that a person has "a heart of stone" to show that the person is not loving. This kind of comparison is called a **metaphor**. Another kind of comparison is a **simile**. For example, a poet might write, "the sea was like a dark green blanket." Similes use the words *like* or *as* to make comparisons. Metaphors do not use *like* or *as*.

Try It Read more of the poem "The Fisherman" by Abbie Farwell Brown.

> They're like the sea on foggy days,—
> Not gray, nor yet quite blue;
> They're like the wondrous tales he tells
> Not quite — yet maybe — true.

Discuss Look back at the first stanza on the previous page. To what does the poet compare the fish? Circle the two things being compared in this metaphor. Look at the stanza on this page. The poet is writing about the fisherman's eyes. To what does the poet compare the eyes? Circle the two things his eyes are compared with in the similes.

As you read, complete the Figurative Language Chart on page 240.

Purpose for Reading

Read along with your teacher. Each time, read for a different purpose.

First Read	Focus on determining the theme.
Second Read	Focus on finding and understanding figurative language.
Third Read	Focus on analyzing the poems.

The Wind Tapped Like a Tired Man

by Emily Dickinson

Read how the poet describes the wind. To what does she compare the wind in each stanza on this page? Circle the things that are compared. Record these comparisons on the **Figurative Language Chart**.

1   The wind **tapped** like a tired man,
    And like a host, "Come in,"
    I boldly answered; entered then
    My residence within

5   A rapid, footless guest,
    To offer whom a chair
    Were as impossible as hand
    A sofa to the air.

How does the poet feel about the wind? How do you know this?

No bone had he to bind him,

10 His speech was like the **push**

Of numerous humming-birds at once

From a superior bush.

His countenance[1] a billow,

His fingers, if he pass,

15 Let go a music, as of tunes

Blown tremulous[2] in glass.

He visited, still flitting;

Then, like a timid[3] man,

Again he tapped—'t was flurriedly—

20 And I became alone.

[1]**countenance** face
[2]**tremulous** shaky
[3]**timid** shy

Think about how the poet describes the wind throughout the poem. What overall message is the poet giving about the wind?

The poet compares the noise of the wind to two different things on this page. Find the two comparisons. Then record them on the **Figurative Language Chart.**

How would you describe the wind's "visit" with the poet? Was it a pleasant experience for the poet or not? Use evidence from the text to support your answer.

Winter

by Walter de la Mare

Think about winter—the weather, animals, and length of the days. What message is the poet giving about winter?

In the first stanza, to what does the poet compare the robin's breast? Record this comparison on the **Figurative Language Chart.**

In the last stanza, the poet writes that there are "frost-fires," or stars, in the sky. To what does the poet compare the stars? Record this comparison on the **Figurative Language Chart**.

Compare

How do both poems present nature? How are the themes of the poems the same? How are they different?

1   Clouded with snow
The cold winds blow,
And shrill on leafless bough
The robin with its burning breast
5   Alone sings now.

The rayless sun,
Day's **journey** done,
Sheds its last ebbing[1] light
On fields in leagues[2] of beauty spread
10   Unearthly white.

Thick draws the dark,
And **spark** by spark,
The frost-fires kindle,[3] and soon
Over that sea of frozen foam
15   Floats the white moon.

[1]**ebbing** fading
[2]**leagues** miles
[3]**kindle** begin to burn

Vocabulary: Choose Words to Convey Ideas Precisely

Poets choose words creatively and carefully. The words they choose convey, or tell, their ideas precisely, or exactly. For example, in "Winter," the poet compares the snow-covered landscape to a "sea of frozen foam." This is a strange comparison, but it is carefully crafted to create a vivid image in your mind.

Try It Read this line from "The Wind Tapped Like a Tired Man."

> The wind **tapped** like a tired man,

The poet uses the word *tapped* to suggest a light touch.

> **Discuss** **Think about how these exact words work together to create an image of the wind. How else could a wind knock on a door? How else could the man be described?**

Find the following words in "The Wind Tapped Like a Tired Man" and "Winter." Tell how the words show exactly what the poet means. Then list some other words the poet could have used that are not as exact.

1. **push,** p. 99 _____

_____

2. **journey,** p. 100 _____

_____

3. **spark,** p. 100 _____

_____

Respond to Text: Compare and Contrast Topics

Two of the poems you read, "The Wind and the Moon" and "The Wind Tapped Like a Tired Man," are about the wind. In both poems, the wind is like a person who speaks and acts with personality. However, each poet describes the wind's personality very differently.

Try It Think about the wind in both of these poems.

> Discuss   **Compare and contrast the wind in both poems. How are the winds similar? How are the winds different?**

On Your Own Write about the two poems you read: "The Wind and the Moon" and "The Wind Tapped Like a Tired Man." Summarize the poems, and tell how each poet describes the wind. Then compare the winds to each other. Use the next page to help you plan your response. Then write your paragraph on a separate sheet of paper.

Checklist for a Good Response

A good paragraph

✔ shows your understanding of what the poems mean.

✔ describes the wind in each poem.

✔ explains how the winds are similar to and different from each other.

✔ includes a topic sentence, supporting ideas, and a concluding statement.

✔ includes complete sentences.

✔ is free of spelling and grammatical errors.

My Comparison of the Topics

1. **Topic Sentence** Include this information in your first sentence:

   The two poems, "The Wind and the Moon" and "The Wind Tapped

   Like a Tired Man," both _____

2. **Detail Sentences** The sentences of your paragraph should provide details about the wind and how they are similar and different in the two poems. Use this chart to organize your ideas.

Poem	Main Idea	Details About Wind	How Winds Are Similar	How Winds Are Different
"The Wind and the Moon"				
"The Wind Tapped Like a Tired Man"				

3. **Concluding Sentence** Your final sentence should restate your topic with a new twist.

   _____

   _____

On a separate sheet of paper, write your paragraph.

Read on Your Own

Read the poem independently three times, using the skills you have learned. Then answer the Comprehension Check questions.

First Read   Practice the first-read skills you learned in this lesson.

Second Read   Practice the second-read skills you learned in this lesson.

Third Read   Think critically about the poem.

A Bird Came Down the Walk

by Emily Dickinson

Visualize Think about where the poet is standing and what she sees.

Elements of Poetry Think about the rhyming words in the poem. Underline the rhyming words in each stanza. The rhyming words in stanza 1 have been underlined for you.

1   A bird came down the walk:
He did not know I <u>saw</u>;
He bit an angle-worm in halves
And ate the fellow, <u>raw</u>.

5   And then he drank a dew
From a convenient grass,
And then hopped sidewise to the wall
To let a beetle pass.

He glanced with **rapid** eyes
10   That hurried all abroad—
They looked like frightened beads, I thought;
He **stirred** his **velvet** head

Figurative Language
The poet writes that the bird's eyes "looked like frightened beads." Think about what the poet is expressing.

Theme Think about the theme of this poem and what the poet is saying about nature.

Critical Thinking Think about why the poet mentions butterflies at the end of the poem.

Like one in danger; cautious,
I offered him a crumb,
15 And he unrolled his feathers
And rowed him softer home

Than oars divide the ocean,
Too silver for a seam,
Or butterflies, off banks of noon,
20 Leap, plashless,[1] as they swim.

[1]**plashless** without splashing

✓ Comprehension Check

1. What is the main message of the poem? What idea about nature does the poet express?

   _____

   _____

   _____

2. Read the poem aloud quietly. Tap the rhythm on your desk. Count the beats in each line. Does the poet use the same rhythm throughout the poem, or does the rhythm change? Explain.

   _____

   _____

   _____

3. How many stanzas does this poem have? In which stanza does the poet tell about the bird drinking dew?

   _____

   _____

   _____

4. Read this line from the second stanza on page 105.

   He stirred his velvet head

   Look at the words *stirred* and *velvet*. Pick one of the words. How does this word help you picture the bird or his actions? What other words could the poet have used? Would these words be better or worse than the word she used? Why?

   _____

   _____

   _____

5. Read these lines from the second stanza on page 105.

   He glanced with rapid eyes
   That hurried all abroad—

   Which word in these lines has a similar meaning to the word *rapid*? Based on this context clue, what does *rapid* mean?

   _____

   _____

6. Read the first stanza on page 106. What does the poet really mean by "And he unrolled his feathers / And rowed him softer home"?

   _____

   _____

   _____

Lesson 5
Historical Nonfiction

Historical nonfiction tells about real events and people from the past. This kind of writing is nonfiction because it is based on facts. It is historical because the events have already happened. People might read historical nonfiction because they want to learn what life was like many years ago. Readers might also want to find out about important events that took place and why they happened. Suppose you read an article about the people in this picture. What would you want to know about them and the time in which they lived?

Skills Focus

Letter from a Chinese Railroad Worker

Main Idea and Details   **Firsthand Account**

Building the Transcontinental Railroad

Summarize   **Secondhand Account**

Practice the Skill

First Read | **Main Idea and Details**

The **main idea** is the most important thing an author wants readers to know. The main idea is usually stated in the first paragraph. The paragraphs that follow contain **supporting details** that explain the main idea. The last paragraph is the conclusion. In it, the author restates the main idea and sums up the details. Recognizing the main idea and supporting details in a historical nonfiction text will help you understand how the events or ideas fit together.

Try It Read this paragraph.

> The Civil War was a turning point in U.S. history. The conflict had a lot to do with the issue of slavery. In the North, most people were against slavery. However, Southerners believed they needed enslaved workers to run their farms and businesses. This difference between the two sides led to a war that nearly tore the country apart.

> Discuss > **What is the main idea of the paragraph? Underline it. Find a detail that supports the main idea. Double underline it.**

Read on to find another example of a main idea.

> People in the South were eager to expand slavery into the new territories in the West. Many Northerners spoke out against this. They wrote newspaper articles about why slavery should not be allowed in the territories. The Northerners were not sure they could stop slavery in the South, but they did not want to see it spread.

> Discuss > **Underline the main idea of the paragraph. Double underline the supporting details.**

As you read, complete the Main Idea and Details Chart on page 241.

Practice the Skill

A **firsthand account** is written by a person who witnessed the events he or she describes. A firsthand account uses the pronouns *I*, *we*, and *us* to tell what the writer saw or experienced. Many firsthand accounts take the form of personal letters, diaries, interviews, or memoirs.

Firsthand accounts are not always accurate or fair. Sometimes, the authors do not have all the facts, so their accounts might be incomplete. These accounts also might be written years after the events took place, after memories have faded. As you read firsthand accounts, ask, "Did the events really happen that way?"

Try It Read this paragraph.

I turned nine in 1893. That year, I had my first ride on the Ferris wheel at the Chicago World's Fair. It was a brand-new invention—a giant wheel with cars hanging from it. At first, I felt a little afraid to try it. But I was curious. My father and I got into one of the cars with a lot of other people. Each car had room for sixty riders! I held my breath when the wheel began to move. When we reached the very top of the ride, I could see the whole city far below. I thought I could see all of Lake Michigan sparkling in the sun. The view was so amazing that I forgot to be afraid anymore!

> **Discuss** **How do you know this is a firsthand account? Circle the words that tell you. What memorable thing happened to the author in 1893, and how did the author feel about the experience? Draw a box around the words that tell you.**

As you read, record your answers to questions about firsthand accounts on the Close Reading Worksheet on page 242.

Purpose for Reading
Read along with your teacher. Each time, read for a different purpose.

First Read Focus on identifying the main idea and supporting details.

Second Read Focus on recognizing features of a firsthand account.

Third Read Focus on evaluating the text critically.

Letter from a Chinese Railroad Worker

This letter is a fictional work about a made-up person that models the characteristics and text features common in authentic texts of this type.

Dear Wife,

What main idea about building the railroad does the author state on this page? Underline it. Double underline a detail that supports it. Write both on the **Main Idea and Details Chart**.

How can you tell this is a firsthand account?

1   As I write this letter on Sunday, July 7, 1867, I realize that so much has happened since I left you back home in China! I must tell you about my adventures in this land of America.

2   I ought to start by saying that California is nothing like Canton, China. For one thing, the people here despise the Chinese and would rather we all return home. But I pay no attention, as I have a good job now, building a railway for the Central Pacific Railroad Company. It is hard and sometimes dangerous work—but very important! The railroad will help make the United States a great nation.

3   Can you believe that the railroad bosses are eager to hire Chinese workers? In fact, we Chinese outnumber the white men by many thousands—and for good reason. The bosses have discovered that we are superior workers!

4   At first, they didn't want to hire us because they considered us too small and weak. Then they saw how tough we were and noticed our skill at building. After all, they should remember that our people built the Great Wall!

5   I doubt anything is worse than trying to build a railroad through the mountains in the winter, but that's what we are trying to do. When it is complete, the track will run across the whole North American continent. That is why they call it the First Transcontinental Railroad. It will stretch from the West Coast all the way to the East Coast. It will allow people and goods to travel great distances faster than ever. There has never been such a thing before, and we Chinese will become famous for building it!

6   The mountains I speak of are the Sierra Nevada. They separate the state of California from the state of Nevada. We have just endured a most severe winter here. The snowdrifts were many feet high, causing us to do more shoveling than laying track. A few men died from the cold, and avalanches buried others. But thankfully, I am still alive, strong, and healthy!

7   My team is working on the east side of the mountains, blasting through solid **granite** to make train tunnels. It is backbreaking work, and our progress is slow. We go forward by less than two feet a day. The bosses expect the Summit Tunnel, called Number 6, to be finished sometime this summer. It has taken two whole years to blast out this tunnel. When it's done, we'll begin laying track down the mountains' eastern side. The work is rough, and I look forward to leaving the Sierras behind.

What details on this page support the idea that building a railroad is hard work? <u>Double underline</u> them. Then write them on the **Main Idea and Details Chart**.

The author of the letter says that a few men died of cold or in avalanches. In fact, more than a dozen men died. Why do you think the author got this fact wrong?

From 1866 through 1868, the Central Pacific's Chinese workers built fifteen tunnels in the Sierra Nevada.

What details on this page support the idea that building a railroad is dangerous work? <u>Double underline</u> them. Then write them on the **Main Idea and Details Chart**.

A firsthand account often expresses the writer's personal opinions. Circle the author's opinions about Chinese workers.

8   The most dangerous part of laying tracks through the Sierra Nevada are the explosions. At first, we used an explosive called black powder, but it was not nearly powerful enough. Progress was very slow. Now we are trying something new. It is called **nitroglycerin**, a very powerful and dangerous chemical. It can blast through rock more quickly than black powder can.

9   Sometimes there are accidents, but my job comes with fewer risks than many others, since I work as a grader. That means I make the land level, so the men behind me can lay the big wooden **railroad ties** and then lay the metal tracks on top of them. Rather than explosives, I use simple hand tools such as picks, shovels, hammers, and drills. Do not doubt that I am very careful!

10   I work on a team of about thirty men, and everyone laboring here works six days a week. We work long shifts that start at sunrise and often end only when the sun sets. That's a long, tiring day. But every evening after work, I take a relaxing sponge bath in hot water. This is another thing our bosses like about the Chinese. We are clean—and we are much more quiet than the white workers, to be sure!

11   We are also proud of how much we accomplish every day. In fact, when we are on flat land, we can lay about three miles of track in a single day. I will tell you for certain that this is more than most other teams do!

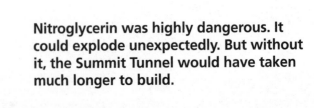

Nitroglycerin was highly dangerous. It could explode unexpectedly. But without it, the Summit Tunnel would have taken much longer to build.

12   Perhaps we Chinese excel because we eat so well. Life here has a few advantages, believe it or not! We hired a cook, and he has many delicious foods brought up to us from San Francisco, such as fresh shellfish, poultry, and Chinese bacon. Of course, we have rice and rice cakes, and sometimes we enjoy salted cabbage or cuttlefish with bamboo sprouts. After a difficult day of work, we are all starving, and our cook takes good care of us.

13   On Sundays, no one works, and the white workers have found all kinds of ways to waste their time. In our Chinese camp, however, things are orderly, and we keep to ourselves. We use our free day to take care of chores. I write my letters and wash and mend my clothes. Wife, you will be satisfied to know that I wear fresh clothing every day, just like I did at home.

Circle the author's opinion about white workers.

Did the positive aspects of the Chinese workers' camp life make up for the hardships they suffered? Why or why not?

Grocers in San Francisco supplied the Chinese railroad workers with familiar foods.

What feelings or attitudes expressed in this account might not appear in a secondhand account? Why?

14   The final thing I must confess to you is about our **workers' strike**. On June 25—only twelve days ago—two thousand of us put down our tools and headed back to camp. We went on strike for good reason. Chinese workers are paid thirty-five dollars a month, from which we must buy all our own food. But the white men working beside us get paid more than we do for doing the same work—and they get free meals besides! Would you consider this fair? No! That is why we stopped our work.

15   So, we demanded forty dollars a month, and we asked for shorter working hours as well—no more than ten hours a day. Another thing we wanted was shorter shifts in the dark, freezing tunnels because a man needs a break from such conditions before too long!

16   When the bosses refused us everything, we did not back down. Instead, we asked for even more—forty-five dollars a month. With that, they cut off all our food and other supplies. For a whole week we remained in camp, but we did not riot. Instead, we held out quietly and hoped for the best.

17   Seven days later, the bosses announced that anyone who continued to strike would lose a whole month's pay. What could we do but give in and return to work? Most of us did, as we desperately need our jobs. A few left to look for other work, but some stayed in camp and continued striking. They were ordered back to the job by white men who aimed guns at them. And so the railroad work goes on.

18   We did not get shorter hours or more money, but I am sure of one thing, dear Wife. Your loving husband will be counted in this country's history. I am one of the soon-to-be-famous transcontinental railroad builders!

Wishing to see you,
Chen Bo

Argue

Was the successful completion of a new national railroad a good reason for the unfair treatment of Chinese workers? Why or why not?

Vocabulary: History Terms

A **history term** is a word or phrase that relates to a historical topic. For example, you might find the word *revolution* in an article about the American colonies' fight for independence. History terms are often shown in bold print or italics. You need to know what these words mean in order to understand the article. Sometimes, a history term is defined in the sentence in which it appears. Other times, you must figure out what the term means by looking for clues in the sentences around it.

Try It Read these sentences from "Letter from a Chinese Railroad Worker."

> The final thing I must confess to you is about our **workers' strike**. On June 25—only twelve days ago—two thousand of us put down our tools and headed back to camp.

Underline the words that help you figure out the meaning of the term *workers' strike*.

▶ Discuss **What can you tell about the meaning of *workers' strike* from the events the author describes?**

The following history terms appear in the selection. Find the terms and their context clues. Then write a definition for each term.

1. **granite**, p. 113 _____

2. **nitroglycerin**, p. 114 _____

3. **railroad ties**, p. 114 _____

Practice the Skill

First Read Summarize

Summarizing is an important reading skill. To **summarize** means to retell in your own words the most important information in a text. When you summarize an article, you include only its main idea and the most important supporting details. That means a summary is much shorter than the original text.

Summarizing a text can help you make sure that you understand what you have read. If you can put its most important points into your own words, you have understood the text and are more likely to remember its main ideas and details.

Try It Read this paragraph.

The Klondike gold rush was North America's last great gold rush. It started when gold was discovered in Canada's Klondike region in 1896. The rush to make a fortune in gold brought about 100,000 people to Canada. But getting to the site of the Canadian gold deposits, mainly along the Klondike River, was not easy. The route was difficult and covered in deep snow. Temperatures were below freezing. People in search of gold had to carry heavy equipment long distances through mountain passes. In the end, less than half of those who wanted to strike it rich even made it to the Klondike region. And very few found enough gold to actually get rich.

⟩ Discuss ⟩ **What is this paragraph mostly about? How would you summarize it if you wanted to quickly give someone the general idea? Underline the points important enough to include in your summary.**

As you read, complete the Summary Chart on page 243.

Practice the Skill

A **secondhand account** is written by a person who did not witness the event he or she is writing about. The writer of a secondhand account finds facts by reading many firsthand accounts, such as personal letters, diaries, interviews, or memoirs. The writer must make judgments about the accuracy of the information. Then he or she draws conclusions about the events and writes them in a secondhand account.

A secondhand account uses pronouns such as *he*, *she*, and *they* rather than *I* and *we*. It takes a wider view of an event than a firsthand account does because it is written when more information has been gathered.

Try It Read these paragraphs.

On May 29, 1953, Sir Edmund Hillary and Tenzing Norgay climbed to the top of Mount Everest. Mount Everest, part of the Himalaya range spanning the countries of Nepal and China, is the highest mountain in the world.

Reaching Mount Everest's peak is difficult and dangerous. At the high altitude near the peak, there is little oxygen, so breathing is difficult. Terrible storms and freezing temperatures add to the problems. There are also few places to find shelter.

Yet, Hillary and Norgay never gave up. Many others had failed to reach Everest's summit, but Hillary and Norgay were the first to reach the top of the world. That day, they made history.

Discuss **How do you know these paragraphs are from a secondhand account? Circle the words that tell you.**

As you read, record your answers to questions about secondhand accounts on the Close Reading Worksheet on page 244.

Purpose for Reading

Read along with your teacher. Each time, read for a different purpose.

First Read Focus on summarizing what you read.

Second Read Focus on describing a secondhand account.

Third Read Focus on evaluating the article critically.

Building the Transcontinental Railroad

Summarize what this page says about how the transcontinental railroad affected cross-country travel in the 1860s. Underline the points that should go in your summary. Restate them in your own words on the **Summary Chart**.

What clues does the author provide to let you know this account was written long after the events it describes?

1   By the early 1860s, the American people were dreaming of a transcontinental railroad that would cross the entire United States. At that time, there were no airplanes, and no trains ran west from the Missouri River, so a cross-country trip was long and difficult.

2   Before the transcontinental railroad was built, to get from the East Coast to the West Coast, you could take a train to Missouri and then hire a **stagecoach** to take you to California. But travel across the "Wild West" was rough and dangerous. If you decided to go by ship, you'd have to sail around the tip of South America and then back north to the United States. Either trip could take six months and would cost nearly $1,000— that's more than $14,000 in today's money.

3   Once the transcontinental railroad was built, the trip from New York to California cost no more than $150 and took about one week.

The Race Begins

4   In 1862, the dream of a transcontinental railroad started to become a reality. That year, President Abraham Lincoln signed a bill called the Pacific Railway Act. The act provided money and land for building the railroad.

5   Two big companies got the job of building the railroad. Together, they would lay the tracks to make a coast-to-coast railway system. The company in charge of building from the east was the Union Pacific Railroad (UP). The Central Pacific Railroad Company (CP) would build from the west.

6   The Pacific Railway Act made the government's expectations clear. The UP was to start building west from the Missouri River. The CP would start in Sacramento, California, and would build east. The CP line would cross through the Sierra Nevada mountain range, and then it would travel down into the flat, dry Nevada desert. At some point, the two companies' train tracks would meet up and be joined together.

7   The terms of the act created the perfect conditions for a competition between the two companies. They would race to see who could lay the most track. The CP got a head start, breaking ground by shoveling the first bit of dirt in January 1863. The UP did not begin serious building until 1865, but it made up for lost time later. The UP was able to lay great lengths of track because it did not face the challenge of crossing the Sierra Nevada.

> Summarize the most important points about the race to build the transcontinental railroad. <u>Underline</u> key words or phrases. Then write your summary on the **Summary Chart**.

> What clues tell you this is a secondhand account? Circle them.

The Union Pacific and the Central Pacific wanted to build the railroad quickly so that the nation would have a better way to transport people and goods across the country.

What is this page mainly about? Restate the most important ideas on the **Summary Chart**.

What kinds of firsthand accounts do you think the author read and researched to get the information for this secondhand account?

The Need for Workers

8   Charles Crocker, one of the four CP directors, had the responsibility of overseeing construction of the CP railroad from the west. But Crocker could not find enough workers. The job required working in scorching sun and blinding blizzards. The days were long and hard, and the pay was low. Many men gave it a try but soon fled.

9   Crocker knew he would not get anywhere without a lot of workers. To stay on schedule, he needed thousands of men, but even on a good day, he usually had no more than about eight hundred on the job.

Calling in the Chinese

10   Chinese **immigrants** were flooding into California at that time, but they faced great racial prejudice. Whites did not want to work with them or live near them. However, Crocker thought they might be well suited to working on the railroad. He presented the idea to James Strobridge, his **foreman**. Strobridge was against the idea of having them on his team, but he finally gave in and agreed to try using Chinese workers.

11   Hiring Chinese workers to build the railroad made a significant difference. The men worked tirelessly under all conditions. They were respectful and orderly, and they did their jobs very well. By 1868, about twelve thousand Chinese were employed—so many that about eight out of every ten railroad workers had been born in China.

Fierce Competition

12   Crocker's crews spent more than a year blasting train tunnels through the Sierra Nevada. The black powder they used for blowing up the rock was expensive, and it didn't do much damage to the hard granite. But in February 1867, they began using a new invention called nitroglycerin. This explosive packed more power and, therefore, saved the crews much time and energy. After it was introduced, their progress wasn't measured in inches but in feet. This was real progress!

13   Meanwhile, the UP railroad workers had been speeding ahead with their portion of the railroad. By mid-1867, they were well ahead of the CP. The UP had laid almost four times as much track by that point. However, they had not had to blast their way through a granite mountain range.

14   Although they were behind, Crocker was proud of his CP railroad crews. He wanted to prove how good they were. The UP directors had challenged him. They offered him $10,000 if his crews could beat the UP record. They said their workers had laid eight miles (12.8 km) of track in a single day. On April 28, 1869, Crocker accepted the challenge. His men set to work, and they worked fast. At the end of twelve hours, they had laid ten miles (16 km) of track!

15   The competition was beyond fierce. In less than two weeks, the two railroad lines would meet up. Both wanted to lay more track and win the competition.

If you were to write a summary of the competition between the two railroad companies, which details would you leave out? Put a box around them.

How did the author know that Crocker was proud of his workers?

Charles Crocker had faith in his workers. As a group, they laid track like a well-oiled machine.

Summarize the completion of the transcontinental railroad in the spring of 1869 on your **Summary Chart**.

Why was the completion of the transcontinental railroad a historic moment? ✏️

Analyze

Besides making travel faster, in what other ways did the transcontinental railroad help the United States? ✏️

The words "The last spike" were engraved on the symbolic golden spike. Both railroads had come a long way to meet in Utah. UP had put down 1,086 miles of track, and CP had put down 690 miles.

A Race to the Finish

16   By spring 1869, the two sets of railroad tracks were nearing the point at which they would meet. The struggle to choose a meeting place for the two lines was intense. For every mile of track the companies laid, they received $48,000 from the government. Each company intended to make the most money possible, so each one wanted the meeting place to be far away from its starting point. After a lot of angry fighting between the two companies, they agreed on a spot. The railroads would connect at a place called Promontory Summit, Utah.

17   On May 10, 1869, CP's workers laid the last tracks to connect the lines. A large crowd of railroad officials, reporters, and local people cheered as a golden **spike** was tapped into the ground. (The golden spike was replaced by a regular spike and stored in a safe place after the ceremony.)

18   Across the United States, the public got the news by telegraph. When the last spike was driven, a message went out that simply said, "DONE." It was a historic moment. The transcontinental railroad was complete. It had been built without the help of steam power, electric tools, or motorized equipment. It came to be only through the physical effort of thousands of hardworking men. The United States was now united in a new way. Having a cross-country railroad meant speedier mail delivery and shipment of goods, and now people could travel and settle across the great land with ease.

Vocabulary: Using a Dictionary

When you see an unfamiliar or difficult word in a history article, you should look it up in a **dictionary**. A dictionary entry will tell you how to define, spell, and pronounce the word. The pronunciation guide will also show you which syllable or word part is stressed.

Sometimes a word has more than one meaning or pronunciation. The dictionary entry will list the word's meanings according to the part of speech and show the different ways to pronounce the word.

Try It Read this sentence from "Building the Transcontinental Railroad." Then read the dictionary entry below it.

> A large crowd of railroad officials, reporters, and local people cheered as a golden **spike** was tapped into the ground.

> **spike** (spīk) *noun.* **1:** a heavy metal nail; *verb.* **2:** to punch

 What tells you how to pronounce *spike*? Which definition fits the way the word is used in the sentence?

The following words appear in "Building the Transcontinental Railroad." Use a dictionary to check their meaning and pronunciation. Then write each word's definition.

1. **stagecoach,** p. 120 _____

2. **immigrants,** p. 122 _____

3. **foreman,** p. 122 _____

Respond to Text: Compare and Contrast

"Letter from a Chinese Railroad Worker" and "Building the Transcontinental Railroad" tell about people and events involved in building the transcontinental railroad across the United States. Some details in the texts are similar, but many are different. The authors had different ideas they wanted to share about the same topic. They also wrote in different time periods.

Try It Think about what you have learned from the texts about the building of the transcontinental railroad.

 Discuss **When you compare and contrast, you look at how two things are the same and how they are different. Which details are the same in both texts? Which details are different? Think about why the authors included different information.**

On Your Own Write a paragraph in which you compare and contrast "Letter from a Chinese Railroad Worker" and "Building the Transcontinental Railroad." Tell how the texts are similar and different. Identify details from the texts. Use the next page to plan your writing. Then write your paragraph on a separate sheet of paper.

Checklist for a Good Response

A good paragraph

✔ states a main idea about similarities and differences.

✔ tells how the two texts are the same or similar.

✔ tells how the two texts are different.

✔ includes evidence from the texts to support your ideas.

✔ shows your understanding of the information.

✔ ends with a concluding statement.

My Comparison and Contrast of the Texts

1. **Topic Sentence** Include this information in your opening sentences:

   Both texts tell about _____.

   But they are different because the letter tells about _____

   _____ ,

   and the article tells about _____.

2. **Detail Sentences** Your paragraph should tell how the texts are similar and different. Use this chart to organize your ideas.

	"Letter from a Chinese Railroad Worker"	"Building the Transcontinental Railroad"	Both
Details			
Type of Account			

3. **Concluding Sentence** Your concluding sentence should sum up your main idea. What important idea do you want readers to learn from

   reading your paragraph? _____

   _____ .

On a separate sheet of paper, write your paragraph.

Read on Your Own

Read the article independently three times, using the skills you have learned. Then answer the Comprehension Check questions.

First Read Practice the first-read skills you learned in this lesson.

Second Read Practice the second-read skills you learned in this lesson.

Third Read Think critically about the article.

The *Vasa*: A Mighty Ship Recovered

Main Idea and Details What main idea about the *Vasa* does the author share on this page? Underline the main idea.

Main Idea and Details What details tell you that the *Vasa* was a beautiful and valuable ship? Circle them. One has already been done for you.

1   A great treasure was brought up out of the Baltic Sea in 1961. It was a Swedish ship called the *Vasa*. Although it was a warship, the *Vasa* had never participated in any battle. It had never even sailed on the open seas. Instead, the *Vasa* had sunk within sight of its dock in 1628 just minutes after its first launch. Then it rested underwater, deep in the mud, for the next 333 years.

2   The *Vasa* was amazingly beautiful, but there was something wrong with its design, which was the reason it sank. It had been built for the Swedish king Gustav II Adolf. The ship was to be a fantastic addition to the Swedish navy's fleet. For two years, many skilled craftsmen worked on the *Vasa*. Carpenters, sail makers, painters, carvers, and other experienced craftsmen did their best to make the ship beautiful in honor of their king.

3   The completed ship was a mighty vessel. The main part of the ship—its bottom, sides, and deck—was called the **hull**. The hull was built from more than one thousand oak trees. The ship was loaded with sixty-four cannons and had ten towering sails. Throughout the ship were hundreds of sculptures covered with thin layers of gold. But the ship, so beautiful to look at, would never sail the open seas.

The Great Launch

4   On August 10, 1628, the *Vasa* was tied to the dock near the king's palace in Stockholm. An excited crowd gathered onshore. People wanted to watch the ship sail away on its first trip, known as its **maiden voyage**. There were about 150 crewmembers and guests on the ship.

5   The captain had to navigate past some high cliffs before the wind would catch the ship's sails and push it out to sea. But as soon as the ship left the shelter of the cliffs, something awful happened.

The *Vasa* Goes Down

6   The *Vasa* began to tilt dangerously. The windows in the sides of the ship, where soldiers would place their guns, were wide open. Water poured into the ship, and it quickly began to sink. Onlookers watched in horror as some crew members dove into the water to escape. Others clung desperately to the ship's ropes as the ship slid under the water.

7   The beautiful warship's first voyage had gone terribly wrong. The ship was less than a mile from shore when it sank. Down went all its treasure and about thirty people. A day of excitement and hope had suddenly turned to one of mourning.

> **Secondhand Account** Think about the details that let you know this account was written many years after the event it describes. Put a box around them.

> **Critical Thinking** Think about how the king probably responded to the news of the sinking of the *Vasa*.

It is not surprising that the *Vasa* sank. The experienced ship designer who began the project became ill, and his less-experienced assistant finished the job.

Summarize What events took place after the *Vasa* was recovered? (Circle) the main events you would include in a summary.

Critical Thinking Think about why it was worth raising and restoring the *Vasa*.

8   At the time, an investigation could not determine why the *Vasa* had sunk. But some things are clear. The ship's design was flawed. The underwater part of the ship was too small. It did not provide enough ballast, or weight, to support the tall masts, or posts that held the sails, and heavy guns. As a result, the *Vasa* was top-heavy and at risk of tipping over in the water. The ship would never have sailed successfully under any conditions.

Recovering the Treasure

9   For hundreds of years, the *Vasa* lay underwater. But it was not forgotten. In 1956, a wreck researcher named Anders Franzen determined its underwater location. Five years later, on April 24, 1961, he and his crew raised the ship from the water. It was damaged, but it could be preserved.

10   Today, the *Vasa* is beautifully restored. The gleaming ship is housed in its own museum in Stockholm and so are the skeletons found in the shipwreck. The museum staff has given them all names, each one beginning with a different letter of the alphabet. The names remind visitors that the skeletons were once living individuals and to treat them with respect.

The *Vasa* Museum, opened in 1990, is on an island in Stockholm, Sweden. It houses the warship and many of its treasures.

✓ Comprehension Check

1. What is the main idea of "The *Vasa*: A Mighty Ship Recovered"?
   Identify two details that support the main idea.

   _____

   _____

   _____

   _____

2. What happened to the *Vasa* after it set off on its maiden voyage?
   Write a summary of the events in your own words.

   _____

   _____

   _____

   _____

3. Based on your reading, who could have given a firsthand account of
   what happened to the *Vasa*?

   _____

   _____

   _____

   _____

4. How might this article be different if it were a firsthand account of the sinking—or the raising—of the ship?

_____

_____

_____

_____

5. Read this sentence from the article.

> **People wanted to watch the ship sail away on its first trip, known as its maiden voyage.**

Circle the words that help you understand the meaning of the history term _maiden voyage_.

6. Read these sentences from the article.

> **The main part of the ship—its bottom, sides, and deck— was called the hull. The hull was built from more than one thousand oak trees.**

Underline the words in the sentence that tell you the meaning of the word _hull_. Where else could you look to find the complete definition of the word and its pronunciation?

_____

_____

_____

Lesson 6

Scientific Nonfiction

Scientific nonfiction gives facts about a science topic. This information might be in a magazine, newspaper, textbook, encyclopedia, or on a Web site. People might read scientific nonfiction for a school project or a job, or just because they are interested in the topic. Suppose you read an article about the fish in this photo. What might you want to learn?

Skills Focus

Coral Reefs: Amazing Ecosystems

Cause and Effect   **Reasons and Evidence**

Sea Horses: Unique Creatures of the Sea

Draw Conclusions   **Text Structure**

Practice the Skill

A **cause** is the reason something happens. An **effect** is what happens as the result of a cause. Scientific nonfiction often explains causes and effects. Read this example from a newspaper article: "As a result of the hurricane, many trees fell." To find the effect, ask, "What happened?" Many trees fell. To find the cause, ask, "Why did it happen?" It happened because of a hurricane.

Notice that connecting words and phrases can signal the link between a cause and an effect. In the example above, *as a result* is a connecting phrase. Other connecting words and phrases include *because*, *if*, *so*, *then*, *after*, *since,* and *therefore*.

However, authors do not always use connecting words to signal a cause-and-effect relationship. Sometimes, you must make the connection between cause and effect on your own.

Try It Read this paragraph.

> All humans burp sometimes. Have you ever wondered why? Air becomes trapped in our stomachs. This can happen when we chew gum, eat too quickly, or drink a bubbly beverage. A burp releases the trapped air.

> Discuss **Think about cause and effect. To find the effect, ask, "What do all humans do?" Circle what humans do (the effect). To find the causes, ask, "Why do we do this?" Underline why it happens (the causes).**

As you read, record your answers to questions about cause and effect on the Close Reading Worksheet on page 245.

Practice the Skill

Authors of scientific nonfiction use reasons and evidence to support the points they make. **Reasons** explain why something is true. **Evidence** is the facts and data that support the reasons.

Read this paragraph: *Many people fear bats and do not want them around. But people should welcome bats because these flying mammals are helpful. Bats eat pests such as mosquitoes that bite humans and spread diseases. Bats also eat insects that destroy farmers' food crops.*

Find the main point that the author makes. Then find the reasons and evidence the author uses to support that idea. In the example above, the author makes the point that people should not fear bats. The author then uses reasons and evidence to explain why bats are helpful.

Try It Read this paragraph.

> Bees and flowers need one another to survive. Bees need flowers for food. They eat the nectar that is found inside flowers. Flowers need bees to make more flowers. Bees collect pollen from flowers and spread it around. That helps more flowers grow.

> Discuss   **Why do bees need flowers? Draw a box around the reason. How does the author support this point? Double underline the evidence that supports the point.**

As you read, complete the Reasons and Evidence Chart on page 246.

Purpose for Reading
Read along with your teacher. Each time, read for a different purpose.

First Read — Focus on looking for cause-and-effect relationships.

Second Read — Focus on how ideas are supported with reasons and evidence.

Third Read — Focus on evaluating the article critically.

Coral Reefs:
Amazing Ecosystems

Why are coral reefs favorite spots for ocean explorers?

What evidence supports the idea that corals are hunters? Write the evidence that supports this point on the **Reasons and Evidence Chart**.

1   Coral reefs are favorite spots for scuba divers, snorkelers, and other ocean explorers. That's no surprise because millions of fascinating sea creatures live on coral reefs. These underwater ecosystems[1] occupy less than 1 percent of the ocean floor. Yet, coral reefs are home to almost 25 percent of all **marine** animals.

2   The corals themselves are as fascinating as the sea life around them. Often, they grow in vivid colors and wild shapes. Many people mistake corals for plants or rocks because they are hard and often grow in plantlike shapes. But corals are animals. Their closest relatives are jellyfish and sea anemones.

What Corals Eat

3   Corals have a close relationship with tiny plants called algae. The algae live inside the corals and use sunlight to make sugar for energy. The corals feast on the algae's energy. But corals don't get all their food from algae. Corals are hunters, too. They have long, stinging tentacles that they use to capture tiny sea creatures for food.

[1]**ecosystems** communities formed by relationships between living creatures and their environment

How Coral Reefs Form

4   A tiny **organism**, or life-form, called a coral polyp[2] attaches itself to the ocean floor. The polyp reproduces and over time becomes a colony of coral polyps. These polyps die, leaving their hard, stony skeletons behind. New polyps form a colony on top of the skeletons. This process repeats itself over and over. After many years, the skeletons form a reef, a ridge of coral near the surface of the ocean.

5   Some coral reefs began forming thousands or even millions of years ago. The Great Barrier Reef is the world's largest coral reef. It stretches for sixteen hundred miles along the northwest coast of Australia. This reef began forming about ten thousand years ago.

Where Coral Reefs Are Found

6   In the United States, coral reefs are found in the Atlantic Ocean, the Caribbean Sea, and around the Hawaiian Islands. Reefs are found along the coasts of more than one hundred other countries worldwide.

7   Most corals need to live in salt water. They grow best in temperatures between 73 degrees Fahrenheit (23 °C) and 84 degrees Fahrenheit (29 °C). Corals—and their algae partners—need sunlight. They cannot grow in deep water where the sun's rays do not reach. Consequently, coral reefs are found mostly in warm, shallow ocean waters.

[2]**polyp** a small aquatic animal with a soft body and a mouth surrounded by tentacles

> Coral reefs are found mostly in warm, shallow water. Underline the causes for this.

> Why do corals need sunlight?

The Great Barrier Reef is the world's largest coral reef and a favorite destination for scuba divers.

What Lives in Coral Reefs?

Why do some people call coral reefs the "rain forests of the sea"?

8   More than one million plant and animal species live in coral reefs. This **biodiversity** is among the greatest on Earth. Some people call coral reefs the "rain forests of the sea." Only rain forests are home to as wide a variety of animals and plants.

9   Coral reefs provide a home to thousands of fish species. Sharks, rays, sea turtles, sponges, lobsters, shrimp, octopuses, snails, worms, and sea stars are among the many other animals that live on coral reefs. Scientists believe that a million or more undiscovered species might live on coral reefs, too!

Coral Reefs and Ocean Health

The author states that "coral reefs are necessary for the health of the ocean." Write the reasons and evidence that support this idea on the **Reasons and Evidence Chart**.

10   Coral reefs are necessary for the health of the ocean. Millions of plants and animals depend on these ecosystems for food and shelter. Without coral reefs, many ocean species would die out.

Why is it important for scientists to know when ocean temperatures or chemical content change?

11   These habitats are also very informative to scientists and others who work to manage and protect ocean life. Coral communities are very sensitive to changes in water temperature. They are also easily affected by changes in the amount of salt and other chemicals in the water. Scientists look to coral reefs for information about water quality. By studying reefs around the world, they can easily tell when human activities or natural events have had an effect on ocean water.

Coral reefs are known for their rich biodiversity.

Why Coral Reefs Are Important

12   Coral reefs are important to humans in many ways. People worldwide depend on coral reefs for protection, air quality, food, and jobs.

13   Protecting life on land, coral reefs can act as a barrier or block between sea and land. They absorb some of the force of big waves and storms at sea. This helps protect land from flooding and other damage.

14   Coral reef ecosystems remove and recycle carbon dioxide from the air. The plants in the reef turn the carbon dioxide into oxygen, which animals and humans breathe. In this way, the reefs act as air purifiers.

15   Fishers depend on coral reefs to earn a living. The fish and shellfish that live in and around coral reefs provide a healthy source of food for many people.

16   Coral reefs are also major tourist attractions. The reefs are a source of learning and excitement for the divers and snorkelers who visit them. Tourism creates jobs for people who work at beach resorts, dive shops, and other businesses.

Coral reefs absorb the force of waves and storms. What effect does this have on land?

The author states that coral reefs are important to humans. Write the reasons and evidence that support this idea on the **Reasons and Evidence Chart**.

Why are coral reefs major tourist attractions?

Many people, such as the owners of dive boats like this one, depend on coral reefs to earn a living.

What causes damage to coral reefs? Underline three causes.

The author states that "10 percent of coral reefs worldwide have been destroyed" and "many more face destruction over the next fifty years." What idea does this evidence support? Record the idea on the **Reasons and Evidence Chart**.

Evaluate

Why is it important to protect coral reefs? What might happen if all coral reefs were destroyed? Use evidence from the article to support your answer.

Coral Reefs in Danger

17   Unfortunately, coral reefs are in danger. Scientists say that 10 percent of coral reefs worldwide have been destroyed already. Experts warn that many more face destruction over the next fifty years.

18   Why is this happening? Pollution is one serious problem. Human activities pollute the ocean with sewage and harmful chemicals. Farming and construction near coastlines cause dirt and chemicals to wash into the ocean.

19   Fishing is another threat. There are environmentally friendly ways to fish. But not everyone fishes in a **sustainable** way. Irresponsible fishing practices, such as using explosives to catch fish, harm fish species and damage the reefs.

20   Climate change also threatens the oceans. Corals cannot live in temperatures above 90 degrees Fahrenheit (32 °C). Therefore, rising ocean temperatures are causing corals to get sick and die.

Protecting Coral Reefs

21   Around the world, many people are working to protect coral reefs. Environmental groups encourage governments to pass laws against pollution and irresponsible fishing. They encourage people not to buy and eat fish caught by destroying coral reefs. They teach tourists how to visit the reefs without damaging the coral. Scientists study the reefs to learn more about how to help them. In some areas, governments have declared coral reef habitats to be sanctuaries. In these areas, human activity is now banned or restricted. With hard work and care, these beautiful and valuable ecosystems will survive.

Vocabulary: Science Terms

A **science term** is an important word or phrase in a scientific nonfiction article. Usually, the word is shown in bold print so it stands out. Often, the definition of the word is either in a footnote at the bottom of the page or in a glossary at the back of the text. If a science term is not defined, you can sometimes use context clues—words, phrases, and sentences around the term—to figure out the meaning.

Try It Read this sentence from "Coral Reefs."

A tiny **organism**, or life-form, called a coral polyp attaches itself to the ocean floor.

If you do not know what the word *organism* means, read the other words in the sentence. Circle the words that help you figure out the meaning of *organism*.

Discuss **Brainstorm definitions of the word *organism*.**

Look for the following science terms in "Coral Reefs." Find the context clues that help you understand what each term means. Write a definition of each term, and use it in a sentence.

1. **marine**, p. 136 _____

_____

2. **biodiversity**, p. 138 _____

_____

3. **sustainable**, p. 140 _____

_____

Practice the Skill

First Read **Draw Conclusions**

When you **draw conclusions**, you combine what you read in a text with what you already know. Drawing conclusions helps you understand information that the author does not directly tell you.

Suppose you read that some ocean plants need sunlight to live, so they cannot live too deep in the ocean. Even if the text did not say it directly, you could draw the conclusion that the sun's rays do not reach deep into the ocean.

A conclusion is a decision you reach after you have thought about what you read. A good conclusion has sound reasoning to support it, including evidence from the text and your own knowledge.

Try It Read these paragraphs from a science article.

> Sharks are in danger. Their population has decreased by 50 percent over the last fifteen years. Overfishing is one big problem for sharks. Fishers accidentally trap sharks in their nets. Other fishers hunt sharks for food or medicine. Also, sharks don't reproduce quickly, so they don't have many offspring.
>
> Fewer sharks means a change in the biodiversity of the ocean. This change could be a disaster for ocean ecosystems. With fewer sharks around to hunt them, some fish populations may explode. Then ecosystems might not provide enough food for all the new fish.

Discuss **What conclusion can you draw about why sharks are important to the ocean? What information helped you draw this conclusion? Place a box around the parts of the text that you used to draw this conclusion.**

As you read, record your answers to questions about drawing conclusions on the Close Reading Worksheet on page 247.

Practice the Skill

Text structure is the way an author organizes ideas and information in a text. The text structure an author chooses depends on the topic and purpose of the text he or she is writing.

Often, authors of scientific nonfiction want to explain why things happen. To do so, they use the cause-and-effect text structure. Remember that a **cause** is the reason something happens, and an **effect** is what happens as a result of a cause. The author may present causes with more than one effect, as well as effects with more than one cause.

Read this sentence, and identify a cause and two effects.

I forgot to shut my bedroom window before it rained, so my carpet got wet, and the books on my windowsill were ruined.

Now identify two causes and their effect in this sentence.

My math book got ruined in the rainstorm, because I left the book on my windowsill and forgot to shut the window.

In addition, an author might use the cause-and-effect text structure to present a cause-and-effect chain. In a cause-and-effect chain, each effect becomes the cause of another effect.

I forgot to shut my window before it rained, so my carpet got wet. The water caused the carpet to get moldy. When my mother saw the mold, she got very angry!

Try It Reread the text about sharks on page 142.

 Discuss **Why are sharks in danger? Why is their population shrinking? Underline three causes in the text. What effects could the decline in sharks have on ocean ecosystems? Circle the effects.**

As you read, complete the Cause-and-Effect Chart on page 248.

Purpose for Reading

Read along with your teacher. Each time, read for a different purpose.

First Read   Focus on drawing conclusions based on details in the article.

Second Read   Focus on examining cause-and-effect text structure.

Third Read   Focus on evaluating the article critically.

Sea Horses:
Unique Creatures of the Sea

The sea horse is a very unusual-looking fish.

1   The sea horse is a strange-looking little fish. It gets its name from its head, which is shaped like a tiny horse's head. The sea horse also has a monkeylike tail, and the male sea horse has a pouch like a kangaroo does.

2   What a sea horse doesn't look like is an ordinary fish. Instead of scales, a sea horse has thin skin. The skin stretches over the sea horse's **unusual** skeleton—a series of bony plates that look like rings or ribs around the sea horse's body. On top of a sea horse's head is a group of spines called a coronet, which gets its name because the spines look like a little crown. Every sea horse has its own unique coronet.

3   A sea horse does not swim the way other fish do, either. Instead of moving horizontally through the water, a sea horse swims in a vertical position. It uses its dorsal fin to move itself forward and its two pectoral fins (one on each side of its body) for steering and balance.

Based on the details in paragraph 2, what do most fish's bodies look like? Draw a box around the evidence that helps you draw this conclusion.

Based on what you have read so far, why is this article subtitled "Unique Creatures of the Sea"?

Sea Horse Variety

4   Scientists have identified thirty-eight species of sea horse. They believe that even more species exist. The pygmy sea horse is the smallest sea horse, at less than one inch tall. The largest sea horse is the Australian big-bellied sea horse, which can grow more than one foot tall.

Where Sea Horses Live

5   Sea horses live in warm, shallow ocean waters. They are found mostly in coral reefs or among sea grass beds. The animals use their long tails to anchor themselves to corals or grasses.

A male sea horse gives birth to its babies.

Sea Horse Babies

6   Here is another way that sea horses are unusual. In most animal species, the females become pregnant and carry the babies, but *male* sea horses perform these roles.

7   How does this work? A female sea horse puts eggs in a male's pouch. The male then fertilizes the eggs. The pregnant male carries the eggs in his pouch for about two to four weeks, after which the baby sea horses are born.

8   Typically, a sea horse dad gives birth to about one hundred to two hundred babies at a time. Smaller species have fewer babies, while some large sea horses can have more than one thousand babies at once! Many or most babies will die before reaching adulthood, however. Often, they are killed by weather conditions such as storms or are eaten by predators.

9   A newborn sea horse is a fully formed, miniature copy of its parents. The newborn is tiny, usually measuring less than a half-inch. A sea horse baby lives on its own from birth. It is not dependent on its parents for care.

Draw a box around the text in paragraph 8 that provides information about the life of a baby sea horse. What do you conclude from this information?

Why do many baby sea horses die before they reach adulthood? Write the two causes on the **Cause-and-Effect Chart**.

Sea Horse Mates

10   Sea horses are unusual in the animal kingdom for another reason, too. Most sea horse species are monogamous. That means that every sea horse has just one mate. Some male-female pairs stay together for years—maybe even for life.

11   The partners in a sea horse pair greet each other every day. They change colors, hold tails, and do a special dance together. After several minutes, the two sea horses split up. They spend the rest of the day apart, finding food.

Hungry Sea Horses

12   Sea horses catch and eat food almost all day long. They are predators, and most eat only live prey. A sea horse doesn't have a mouth or teeth; instead, it uses its tube-shaped snout to suck prey from the water into its body. Because a sea horse also has no stomach, food passes through its digestive system very quickly. Therefore, a sea horse must eat a large amount of food in order to get enough nutrition.

13   A sea horse does not swim to capture its prey. Instead, it catches it ambush-style, waiting quietly until the prey comes close enough to suck it in. Most animals' eyes move together, but a sea horse can move each eye **independently**. That means a hungry sea horse can look for prey in two different directions at once.

14   A sea horse will eat almost anything that fits through its snout. Mostly, it eats tiny crustaceans, or shellfish, but it will also eat newly hatched fish. One sea horse can suck up as many as three thousand tiny shrimp in one day.

Based on the information in "Sea Horse Mates," what conclusion can you draw about the mating practices of other animals?

Why does food pass through a sea horse's digestive system so quickly? Examine the cause-and-effect chain. List the cause and effect on the **Cause-and-Effect Chart**.

A male sea horse carries the eggs in a pouch.

A sea horse is excellent at blending in with its surroundings.

Sea Horse Defense Systems

15   Many fish are expert swimmers, but not sea horses—they are rather **incompetent**. Because they swim upright and have fewer fins than other fish, sea horses don't swim fast or well. Instead, these creatures are masters of camouflage. Their skin changes color to blend in with their surroundings. Sea horses can even grow hairlike skin filaments that look like sea plants and grasses. Sea horses may not be able to escape predators by swimming, but they can hide.

16   Sometimes, predators do catch sea horses. Sea horses have been found in the stomachs of tuna, crabs, sharks, and rays. Still, storms at sea probably kill more sea horses than predators do. A sea horse uses its tail to anchor itself to corals and grasses. Still, storms can rip the sea horse loose. Consequently, some sea horses wash ashore, while others die from exhaustion as they struggle against violent seas.

Sea Horse Mysteries

17   Marine experts are quick to admit that they don't know everything about these fish. For instance, no one knows how many sea horses exist in the oceans. No one is sure how long wild sea horses live, either. The lifespan of a sea horse in an aquarium is about two to three years. But scientists have yet to discover how long sea horses live in the wild.

Based on the details in paragraph 15, why does a sea horse use camouflage? Draw a box around the evidence that helps you draw this conclusion.

How do storms kill sea horses? Examine the cause-and-effect chain. List the cause and effects on the **Cause-and-Effect Chart**.

Why might experts still have unanswered questions about sea horses?

Some people make and sell souvenirs using dried sea horses.

List one cause and one effect of the sea horses' habitat loss on the **Cause-and-Effect Chart**.

Analyze

What do experts mean when they say that saving sea horses means saving the oceans? How might protecting sea horses help oceans?

Sea Horses in Trouble

18   Today, sea horses are at risk. Conservationists have listed several species as threatened. Humans are the biggest threat to these creatures. Fishers sometimes catch sea horses in their nets accidentally. They also catch sea horses **deliberately** for three main purposes.

- Sea horses are used in many traditional medicines. Some people think sea horses can help cure a wide range of medical conditions.

- Other people want live sea horses to keep as pets. Yet, sea horses usually do not do well in home aquariums.

- Some people use dried sea horses to make key chains, jewelry, and other souvenirs.

19   Human activity has also led to habitat loss—another threat to these fish. When coral reefs and sea grass beds are damaged or destroyed, the sea horses that live there die, too.

Saving Sea Horses

20   In 1996, the sea horse expert Amanda Vincent founded Project Seahorse. This group studies sea horses and works to protect these animals and the habitats where they live. Vincent and her team educate people about sea horses. They encourage sea horse fishers to limit their fishing to sustainable levels and have helped to establish laws about buying and selling sea horses. Project Seahorse is also involved in protecting coral reefs. Vincent and other experts believe that saving sea horses means saving Earth's oceans.

Vocabulary: Antonyms

Antonyms are words that mean the opposite of each other. For example, *healthy* and *sick* are antonyms, and *dangerous* and *safe* are antonyms. Knowing a word's antonym can help you understand its meaning. Authors sometimes use antonyms to help readers better understand a description or explanation in the text.

Try It Read this sentence from "Sea Horses."

> Many fish are expert swimmers, but not sea horses—they are rather **incompetent**.

If you do not know what *incompetent* means, look for its antonym—a word that describes what kind of swimmers sea horses are **not**. Double underline the antonym. How does knowing the meaning of *expert* help you understand the meaning of its antonym, *incompetent*?

> Discuss **Brainstorm other antonym pairs that you can use to describe how sea horses swim. Use them in a sentence like the one above.**

Find the following words in "Sea Horses." Look for a nearby antonym that helps you understand what each word means. Then write your own definition on the lines.

1. **unusual,** p. 144 _____

2. **independently,** p. 146 _____

3. **deliberately,** p. 148 _____

Respond to Text: Use Information from Two Texts

"Coral Reefs: Amazing Ecosystems" and "Sea Horses: Unique Creatures of the Sea" both discuss some ways that human activities harm coral reefs and the creatures that live on them.

Try It Think of some facts about this topic that you learned from each text.

 Discuss **What can people do to help protect ocean life? Remember that your ideas should be supported by facts and evidence from both of the texts you have read in this lesson.**

On Your Own Write one or two paragraphs about the ways that human activity harms coral reef ecosystems and what people can do to protect them. Include evidence from each text. Use the next page to help you plan your response. Then write your paragraph(s) on a separate sheet of paper.

Checklist for a Good Response

A good paragraph

✔ states your ideas.

✔ explains the reasons for your ideas.

✔ includes evidence from both texts to support your ideas.

✔ shows your understanding of the information in both texts.

✔ includes a topic sentence, supporting ideas, and a concluding statement.

My Information from Both Texts

1. **Topic Sentence** Include this information in your first sentence:

   "Coral Reefs: Amazing Ecosystems" and "Sea Horses: Unique

   Creatures of the Sea" explain that _____ harms

   coral reef ecosystems and that people can protect them by

   _____ .

2. **Detail Sentences** The sentences of your paragraph(s) should provide
   details that explain your ideas. Use this chart to organize your ideas.

Ways That People Are Harming Coral Reef Ecosystems	Ways That People Can Protect Them

3. **Concluding Sentence** Your final sentence should restate your ideas
   with a new twist.

   _____

   _____

   _____

On a separate sheet of paper, write your paragraph(s).

Killer Plants!

Cause and Effect
Think about why carnivorous plants eat animals. Underline the causes. The first cause has been underlined for you.

Draw Conclusions
Think about why most plants are not carnivores. What kind of soil might they live in?

1   You probably know that sharks are **carnivores**. You know that lions, tigers, and bears are meat eaters, too. But have you ever heard of a meat-eating plant? It may sound strange, but it is true. Some plants are carnivorous.

2   Carnivorous plants are unusual. A **typical** plant does not eat animals. In fact, most plants do not really eat at all. They are neither carnivores—meat eaters—nor herbivores—plant eaters.

3   Instead, plants get their energy from the sun. They convert sunlight into energy through a process called photosynthesis. To carry out this process, plants use energy from the sun, carbon dioxide from the air, and water from the soil to make food for themselves. Soil also provides nutrients for plants.

Catching Prey

4   Like all plants, carnivorous plants convert energy from the sun. So they need nutrients. But most carnivorous plants live in areas where the soil is thin, rocky, or otherwise low in nutrients. These plants get nutrients by luring small animals into traps—and digesting them. These plants eat insects and sometimes even small mammals or reptiles!

5   A plant must meet three criteria to be carnivorous. First, the plant can trap prey. Second, it can digest prey. And third, the plant uses nutrients from the digested prey.

6   Carnivorous plants fall into five categories, based on how they trap their prey.

Snap Traps

7   Plants with snap traps have jawlike leaves that snap shut to trap prey. Trigger hairs grow on the leaves. When prey touches the hairs, the leaves snap shut. Digestive juices inside the leaves break down the trapped prey so that the plant can absorb the nutrients.

8   The Venus flytrap, which uses a snap trap, is the world's most famous carnivorous plant. This plant has been featured in movies, on TV shows, and even in video games.

Sticky Traps

9   Some plants produce a sticky, gluelike substance to trap insects. Sundews are the most numerous of these plants. They include more than one hundred species and live on every continent except Antarctica. The "dew" that gives sundews their name isn't really dew. It's the glue on their prey-grabbing tentacles!

Reasons and Evidence The author states that the Venus flytrap is the world's most famous carnivorous plant. <u>Double underline</u> the evidence that supports this point.

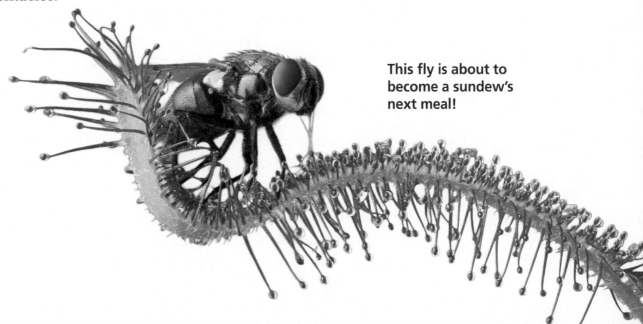

This fly is about to become a sundew's next meal!

This pitcher plant is actually big enough to catch and digest a lizard!

Text Structure
Circle the effects of the leaves and hairs on prey that approaches a plant with a corkscrew trap.

Critical Thinking
Think about why people like to keep carnivorous plants in their homes.

Pitfall Traps

10   Pitfall traps are cup-shaped leaves with liquid at the bottom. Pitcher plants, which have pitfall traps, catch animals inside a rolled-up leaf that looks something like a water pitcher. Once an animal falls in, it can't get out. The "pitcher" contains digestive enzymes that break down the trapped prey into food.

11   Various species of pitcher plants live in North and South America and Australia. Most eat a diet of mainly insects, but some larger species eat small mammals and reptiles.

Corkscrew Traps

12   Corkscrew traps are similar to the pitfall traps found in pitcher plants. However, the underground leaves that make up these traps are shaped more like a Y. Prey that comes too close can't find its way out. Special hairs on the leaves quickly sweep the prey in only one direction—right toward the plant's digestive enzymes! There, the prey is broken down.

Suction Traps

13   Only bladderwort plants have suction traps. Most bladderworts live in bodies of water. They have saclike leaf bladders filled with liquid. A water insect swims past and brushes against a trapdoor on the leaf bladder. The door opens, and the liquid inside the leaf bladder begins to swirl. The swirling whirlpool sucks in the insect. Trapped!

Killer Plants at Risk

14   Many people like to collect carnivorous plants from the wild. They keep or sell the plants as houseplants. This is unfortunate for the plant species. Because of overcollection and habitat loss, some wild species are now endangered. Carnivorous plants may be tough hunters, but they need humans to help protect them and their habitats.

✅ Comprehension Check

1. Why do carnivorous plants eat animals?

    _____

    _____

    _____

2. The author says that pitfall traps and corkscrew traps are similar.
    What evidence supports this point?

    _____

    _____

    _____

3. What conclusion can you draw about the water that bladderwort
    plants grow in? Include evidence from the text to support your
    conclusion.

    _____

    _____

    _____

4. Read these sentences from the article.

   You probably know that sharks are carnivores. You know that lions, tigers, and bears are meat eaters, too.

   Circle the words that help you understand the meaning of the word *carnivores*.

5. Read these sentences from the article.

   Carnivorous plants are unusual. A typical plant does not eat animals.

   Circle the word that is an antonym of *typical*. How does the author's use of antonyms help you understand carnivorous plants?

   _____

   _____

   _____

   _____

6. Why does the cause-and-effect text structure work well for this article?

   _____

   _____

   _____

   _____

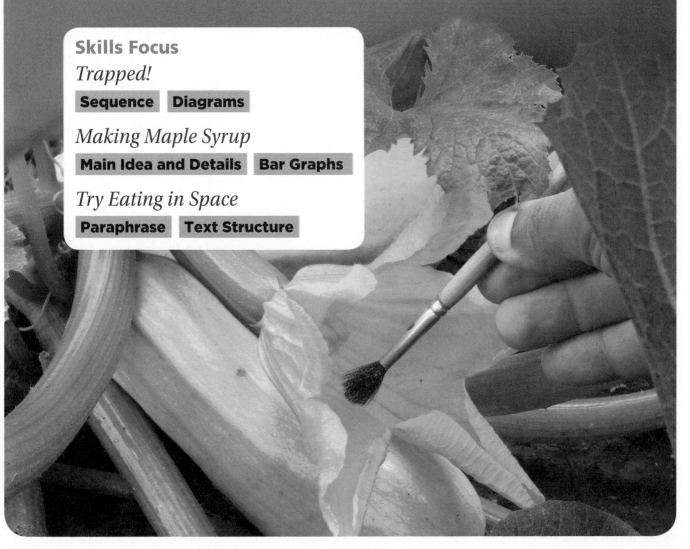

Lesson 7

Technical Texts

Technical texts provide information about science or technology topics and use terms with meanings specific to those topics. They explain what happens and why it happens, or they describe how to do something or how something works in step-by-step order. For example, you might read an article about how a gardener, like the one in the photo below, pollinates flowers. What kind of information do you think you might learn?

Skills Focus

Trapped!

Sequence   Diagrams

Making Maple Syrup

Main Idea and Details   Bar Graphs

Try Eating in Space

Paraphrase   Text Structure

Practice the Skill

Sequence is the order in which things happen. Technical texts often describe a series of events or steps in a process. The order of steps is important so that the procedure works or the product comes out right. For example, an article about how photo lab technicians print pictures would include steps in the printing process.

You can look for clue words that tell about the sequence. Words like *first*, *next*, *then*, and *finally* signal the order in which things happen.

Try It Read this paragraph.

An igloo is a snow house that looks like a ball cut in half. Here's how people make one. First, they mark off a circle in the snow and dig blocks of snow from the area inside it. The snow needs to be deep and tightly packed. Next, they place the blocks around the edge of the circle. They layer the blocks of snow, trimming them so that they lean in toward the center. Then, when the walls are high enough to form a dome, they place a block in the center to close the space at the top. Finally, they create an entrance by digging a hole in the shape they want and covering it with ice blocks. This is how they get in and out of the house.

> **Discuss** Think about sequence to help you understand how to build an igloo. Look for clue words that help you figure out the order of the steps in the paragraph. Double underline the clue words.

As you read, complete the Sequence Chart on page 249.

Practice the Skill

Second Read **Diagrams**

   Technical texts use visuals to help explain information or show a process. One type of visual information is a diagram. A **diagram** is a drawing that shows the parts that make up something or how something works. A diagram usually has a title, labels, and a caption. The **title** says what the diagram is about. The **labels** name parts of the drawing, while the **caption** gives more information about what is shown. For example, a diagram of a rain forest would show the different levels that plants grow to, with each level labeled. A caption would give more information about each level.

Try It Look at this diagram.

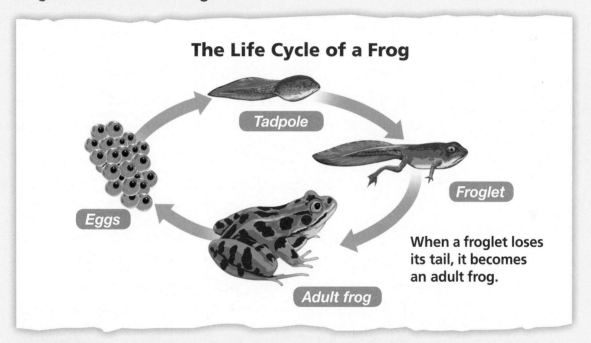

The Life Cycle of a Frog

Tadpole

Froglet

Eggs

When a froglet loses its tail, it becomes an adult frog.

Adult frog

> **Discuss** **Underline the title of the diagram. Circle the labels that name the stages in the life cycle of a frog. Draw a box around the caption that gives information about when a froglet becomes an adult frog.**

As you read, record your answers to questions about diagrams on the Close Reading Worksheet on page 250.

Purpose for Reading
Read along with your teacher. Each time, read for a different purpose.

First Read   Focus on understanding the sequence of events.

Second Read   Focus on using diagrams.

Third Read   Focus on evaluating the article critically.

Trapped!

In what way are people the greatest threat to whales?

1   Whales are large, powerful animals. In fact, blue whales and humpback whales are the largest animals on Earth. So you might think that these giants would be safe from most types of danger. Unfortunately, that's not true.

2   Whales face many threats to their survival. Long ago, people all over the world began to hunt and kill whales. They called this whaling. The whales provided valuable products, like oil and whalebone, that were used for important things like lighting and clothing. But whaling greatly reduced the whale populations. Eventually, people realized that whales were in danger of dying out. They began to work to protect whales and other ocean animals. As a result, laws were passed that made whaling illegal.

3   However, whaling isn't the only threat to whales. When whales swim, rest, or look for food in coastal areas, ships may crash into them. Although this happens by accident, it is still a big problem. Another threat is that polluted, or dirty, waters can poison whales. Fish may die, too, which reduces the whales' food supply.

What Is Entanglement?

4   When people visit the northeastern coast of the United States, they may go on a whale watch. A whale watch takes people out into the ocean for the purpose of seeing whales. If the tourists are lucky, they'll get to see right whales and humpback whales **breaching**, or leaping out of the water.

5   Unfortunately, there is also a large fishing industry in this region. As a result, workers put many fishing lines and lobster traps in the cold waters there. Accidents can happen when the whales get trapped in the fishing gear.

6   When a whale swims into waters where fishing lines and ropes exist, it risks becoming tangled or tied up. This is called **entanglement**. Entanglement is a very serious problem. The ropes work like a trap. When a whale becomes caught in the ropes, it often can't swim, eat, or even breathe. If the ropes wrap around the whale very tightly, they can cut into its skin. The cuts can get infected and cause the whale to die. Even if a whale is able to free itself, pieces of rope may stay attached to its body. This can be dangerous for the whale.

What grows on the heads of right whales? Circle the word in the label and in the caption.

What part is at the tail end of the right whale? Circle the word in the diagram.

Why is going on a whale watch a popular activity?

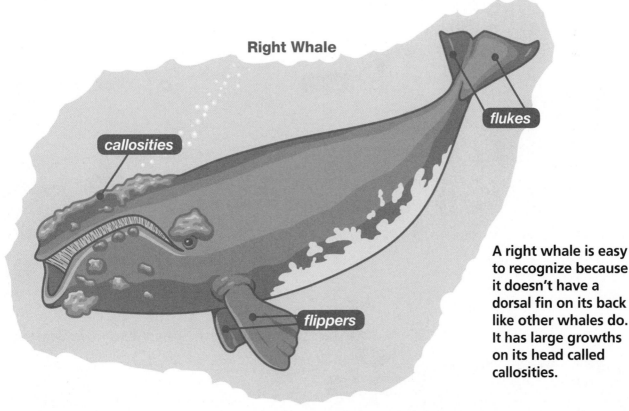

Right Whale

callosities

flukes

flippers

A right whale is easy to recognize because it doesn't have a dorsal fin on its back like other whales do. It has large growths on its head called callosities.

How Does Entanglement Happen?

How can lobster traps harm a whale? Circle the text in the diagram that tells you.

7   Sometimes, fishing ropes wrap loosely around the whales, and they are able to free themselves. But often they can't.

8   Lobster traps are connected to one another by lines or ropes and are lowered into the ocean. The lines are attached to an endline that leads to a buoy, or float, on the surface. When whales swim into this area, they can easily become tangled or trapped in the ropes. The ropes can get stuck in a whale's mouth or wrap around its flippers or tail. Look at the diagram below. It shows how whales can swim into the lobster lines and get tangled up.

9   Scientists found out that more and more whales were being trapped in fishing gear, so they developed methods for freeing the whales. One place where this work is done is the Center for Coastal Studies in Provincetown, Massachusetts. In 1984, workers there developed a plan for freeing the whales. Since then, they have freed many whales. The team at the center is the only one on the East Coast of the United States that is approved to disentangle, or free, the whales from ropes.

A whale can get entangled in floating ropes attached to lobster traps.

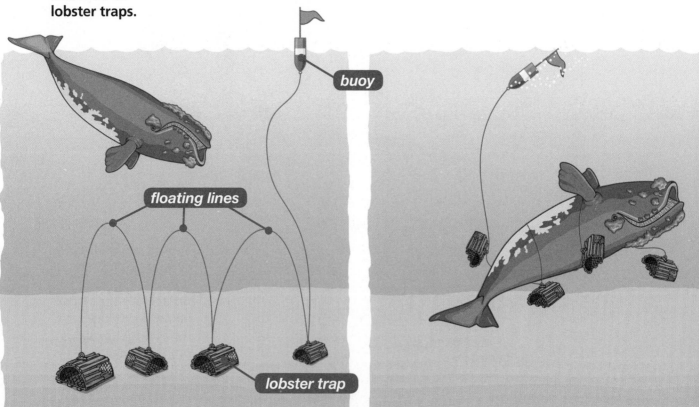

buoy

floating lines

lobster trap

How Are the Whales Freed?

10   When the center hears about a whale in danger, its team goes into action. The first step is to check and see how serious the entanglement is and what the weather conditions are like. Workers must decide if the conditions are right for a rescue. Bad weather makes it more difficult to help a trapped animal and can be dangerous for the rescuers, too.

What do rescuers do first when they learn of an entanglement? Write the answer on the **Sequence Chart**.

11   Next, the rescue team might attach **transmitters** to a buoy, which is connected to the ropes that are trapping the animal. This type of equipment sends signals and allows workers to track the whale's movement and location in the ocean.

Find the sequence word in paragraph 11. What is the second step in the rescue process? Write the answer on the **Sequence Chart**.

12   Then, the rescuers try to get the whale to settle down and stay still. They use a method called **kegging**. The rescuers attach kegs, or barrels, to the ropes around the whale. The kegs keep the whale afloat and prevent it from diving or moving away. Kegging tires the whale, and a tired whale is more likely to stay still while workers try to free it.

Find the sequence word in paragraph 12. What is the third step in the rescue process? Write the answer on the **Sequence Chart**.

13   Finally, the rescuers are ready to cut the lines that have trapped the whale. They have to work very carefully. They do not want to hurt the whale or themselves as they make the cuts. Workers also make sure that they cut all the lines. If they don't, the whale might swim off with pieces of line still attached to it, and that can cause problems for the animal later on.

Find the sequence word in paragraph 13. What is the last step in the rescue process? Write the answer on the **Sequence Chart**.

14   Other animals may also receive help from the rescue team. While rescuers are working to save a whale, they might find dolphins, porpoises, seals, and sea turtles that have become entangled. These animals are lucky if the team members find them when out on a mission.

What Are the Dangers and Solutions?

In what way does entanglement present dangers to people as well as whales?

15   Freeing whales can be a tricky business. Rescue workers can be injured if they collide with a whale. They also risk getting caught in the fishing lines. And it's dangerous for human beings to be in frigid ocean waters for any length of time. So rescue workers must carefully check out each situation. Once they have all the facts, they can decide if the conditions are safe enough for them to continue with a rescue.

16   Because entanglement can be a danger for both the whales and the rescue workers, scientists have a new goal. They want to prevent these accidents from happening in the first place. One way to achieve this is to change the way fishing lines and lobster traps are used. People in the fishing industry, scientists, and government officials have been working together on this problem and have made two important suggestions. First, fishing lines should be made of better material—strong enough to do the job, but weak enough to break if a whale brushes against them. Second, fishing lines should stay on the ocean floor instead of floating in the water.

17   Rescue workers have successfully saved many whales. Hopefully, in the future, fewer whales will become trapped.

Support

How does the article support the idea that solutions to big problems often require cooperation from many different people?

This whale was injured by a fishing line.

Vocabulary: Technology Terms

A **technology term** is one that is important to understanding a particular topic in a technical text. You will find these words in textbooks and articles. The words are often printed in bold, or dark, print.

Try It Read this sentence from "Trapped!"

> If the tourists are lucky, they'll get to see right whales and humpback whales **breaching**, or leaping out of the water.

Discuss In this sentence, the author provides a meaning for *breaching*—"leaping out of the water." If the definition does not appear in the text, you can sometimes use context clues to help you figure out the meaning. For example, in the sentence "You can crop the picture to cut out the unknown people on the side," the context clues for *crop* are "cut out" and "unknown people."

The following words are used in "Trapped!" Find the words in the article, and look for context clues that help you understand their meaning. Write a definition for each word, and use it in a sentence.

1. **entanglement,** p. 161 _____

_____

2. **transmitters,** p. 163 _____

_____

3. **kegging,** p. 163 _____

_____

Practice the Skill

First Read **Main Idea and Details**

The **main idea** is the most important idea in a selection. It tells what the selection is mostly about. **Supporting details** are the pieces of information that support, or tell more about, the main idea. Supporting details tell who, what, when, where, how, or why something happens. For example, the main idea of a paragraph might be that it is important to take care of pets. Details could include when to feed them, how to exercise them, and why you should play with them.

Every selection has a main idea. Each paragraph has a main idea, too. The main idea might or might not be stated directly in the text. If the main idea is not stated, you must think about what the selection or paragraph is mostly about.

Try It Read this paragraph.

> Bamboo is a very useful plant. It's an important source of food for both people and animals. People eat the young shoots and seed of the plant. Pandas eat shoots, leaves, and stems. The giant pandas of China eat bamboo all day long. Bamboo is also a strong building material. It is used to make homes in China. It is also used to make furniture, toys, and cooking tools. It's even used to make clothing!

> Discuss

Think about the main idea and supporting details. Ask yourself, "What is this paragraph mostly about?" Look for the main idea, and circle it. Then ask yourself, "What details tell me more about the main idea?" Underline the details.

As you read, complete the Main Idea and Details Chart on page 251.

Practice the Skill

Second Read Bar Graphs

Another type of visual information used in technical texts is a bar graph. A **bar graph** uses narrow columns of different lengths to show information. This type of graph is used to display or compare different amounts. For example, you could use a bar graph to show the favorite foods of all the students in a class. The highest bar would show the most popular food, and the lowest bar would show the least popular food.

A bar graph usually has a title that explains the purpose of the graph. It also has numbers that help you understand what each bar shows and labels that explain what is being compared.

Try It Look at this bar graph.

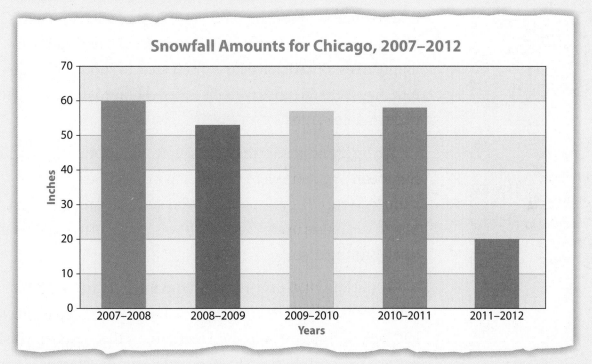

Snowfall Amounts for Chicago, 2007–2012

Discuss What is the title of the bar graph? For what years does the bar graph show snowfall amounts? Which time period had the least amount of snow? Draw a box around the bar that shows you this amount.

As you read, record your answers to questions about bar graphs on the Close Reading Worksheet on page 252.

Purpose for Reading
Read along with your teacher. Each time, read for a different purpose.

First Read — Focus on finding main ideas and details.

Second Read — Focus on using bar graphs.

Third Read — Focus on evaluating the article critically.

Making Maple Syrup

What is the main idea of paragraph 3? Write the main idea on the **Main Idea and Details Chart**.

Which details support the main idea in paragraph 3? Write the details on the **Main Idea and Details Chart**.

1 No one really knows when and where people discovered how to make maple syrup and sugar. Myths tell how Native Americans in North America learned about **sap** running in maple trees. But we have no written facts to support the idea that they were the ones who discovered how to use the sap to make maple syrup.

2 We do know that by the 1700s, both Native Americans and European explorers were boiling sap in large, heavy kettles to make syrup. They also made solid chunks of maple sugar. Maple sugar was useful because it was easy to carry and would last for a long time.

3 By the late 1860s, the maple syrup industry had begun. Farmers would make syrup for their families and sell what was left over. By this time, they had better tools that made the task easier. For example, farmers had metal **spouts** they could put into maple trees. Sap would pour out of the spouts. They also had metal containers in which to collect the sap.

Sugar maples in the fall

Weather and Production

4   Maple syrup is produced where maple trees grow and the weather is favorable. Canada and parts of the northern United States have both the maple trees and the right type of weather. As a result, they are the countries that produce the most maple syrup.

5   Since the weather is not exactly the same every year, some years are better than others for making maple syrup. For example, the 2011 season was great for syrup production. That year, the United States produced almost 2.8 million gallons of syrup. Vermont produced more than 1 million gallons, more than any other state. New York was second, and Maine was third in syrup production.

6   The 2012 season was not as good. In the winter of 2011 to 2012, the weather conditions were very unusual, and late winter temperatures were much warmer than normal. This weather affected how the sap ran in maple trees. Less syrup was produced in the spring of 2012 than in the season before. Some maple syrup producers even decided not to tap their trees and gather sap to make maple syrup. The United States produced less than 2 million gallons of syrup. Vermont produced 750,000 gallons, much less than what was produced the year before.

Use the bar graph to figure out which state produced the greatest amount of maple syrup in 2012. How much syrup was produced?

Use the bar graph to figure out which two states produced about the same amount of maple syrup. How many gallons did each of these states produce?

Why do you think the 2011 season was great for syrup production?

Syrup Production, 2012

Bar graph showing Thousands of Gallons (y-axis, 0 to 800) by States (x-axis):
- Maine: 350
- New Hampshire: 75
- Ohio: 100
- New York: 350
- Vermont: 750

What is the main idea of paragraph 10? Write the main idea on the **Main Idea and Details Chart**.

Which details support the main idea in paragraph 10? Write the details on the **Main Idea and Details Chart**.

Look at the bar graph. In which year was the least amount of syrup produced in Wisconsin?

The state of Wisconsin has sugar maples and weather that are favorable for syrup production.

Trees and Sap

7   Several types of maple trees produce sap. Sugar, black, silver, and red maples are the ones used most frequently. The sap from sugar maples generally has more sugar than the sap from other trees.

8   Maple trees have trunks that are made up of several layers. Sapwood is the layer in which water moves up from the roots to the leaves. During late summer and fall, maple trees begin to store a substance called starch in the sapwood layer. The starch stays in the sapwood as long as the air temperature is colder than 40 degrees Fahrenheit. When air temperatures go above 40 degrees, the starches are changed to sugar. The sugar then moves into the tree's sap.

9   As the seasons change and winter becomes spring, air temperatures rise. Higher temperatures cause **pressure** to build inside the trees. The pressure makes the sap flow, or move in a steady and continuous way. The sap usually flows for about three to six weeks.

10   Air temperature continues to affect the flow of sap. Sap flows best when nighttime temperatures go below freezing, or 32 degrees Fahrenheit. Daytime temperatures should be warmer than 40 degrees. The rise and fall of temperatures is required for sap to continue to flow for several weeks.

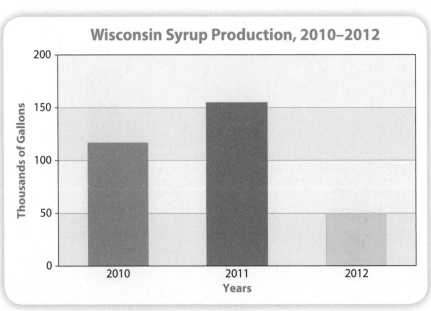

Wisconsin Syrup Production, 2010–2012

How Maple Syrup Is Made

11   Many people living in syrup-producing states collect sap and produce syrup. They follow the process below to make syrup.

Why might it be a good idea to have a cover on the bucket?

12   Workers find maple trees that have a trunk that is at least ten inches in diameter. In each tree they drill a hole that is almost one-half inch wide and about two inches deep. This process is called tapping. They are careful to make sure that the hole is tipped down a bit so that the sap will flow out easily.

13   Next, workers place a spout with a hook into the hole. It's important that the spout is in tight enough so it can't be pulled out easily, but not so tight that it cracks the tree. Then they hang a metal or plastic bucket with a cover on the hook.

14   As soon as the sap starts to flow, workers prepare to boil it. They use a large pot and an outdoor stove or fireplace to boil the sap. When they have enough sap to almost fill the pot, they place it over the fire. They are careful not to fill it too high, or the sap might boil over.

Number of Taps Per Tree	
Width of Tree in Inches	**Number of Taps**
10–17	1
18–24	2
25 or more	3

This chart shows how workers use the size of a tree to figure out how many taps they can safely put into it.

Why should you put an open jar of maple syrup into the refrigerator?

15   As the sap boils down, more is added to the pot. If there is less than two inches of sap in the pot, it might burn. The buckets are checked daily, and more sap is added. Workers take turns watching the pot, since sap can quickly boil and burn.

16   The sap becomes maple syrup when it reaches 7.1 degrees above the temperature of boiling water. A tool such as a candy **thermometer** is used to measure the temperature of the boiling sap.

17   When the syrup reaches the right temperature, it is strained to remove any tiny pieces of sugar. To do this, syrup is poured through clean material, such as wool. The hot syrup is poured into clean containers and sealed. Syrup should be stored in a cool, dry place. Once a jar of syrup is opened, it should be kept in the refrigerator.

Defend

Use information from the article to defend the idea that having a successful maple syrup business depends on the cooperation of nature.

18   Larger businesses are able to produce greater amounts of syrup. To do this, they tap many trees and attach a tube to the spout on each tree. Sap flows out the spout and through the tube. It is collected in one central bin. The sap is put into special pans that are attached to a heat source. Gradually, water in the sap evaporates, or turns into a gas in the air. Soon the sap turns into the delicious, thick syrup that you put on pancakes.

Vocabulary: Reference Materials

Two reference materials you can use to help you learn about words are a dictionary and a glossary. A **dictionary** is a book in which words are listed alphabetically with their meanings, pronunciations, and other information. A **glossary** is an alphabetical list of difficult words or technical terms and their meanings. It can usually be found at the end of a book. If you come across an unknown term in a technical text, you would first look it up in the glossary. If there is no glossary or you cannot find the term there, then check a dictionary.

Try It Read this sentence from "Making Maple Syrup."

> Higher temperatures cause **pressure** to build inside the trees.

If you do not know what the word *pressure* means, look it up in a dictionary. Decide which meaning is being used in the sentence.

Discuss **Brainstorm using other meanings of *pressure* in sentences.**

Find these words in the article. Look up each word in a dictionary to find out what it means. Write the definition of the word as it is used in the article. Then use each word in a sentence.

1. **sap,** p. 168 _____

_____

2. **spouts,** p. 168 _____

_____

3. **thermometer,** p. 172 _____

_____

Practice the Skill

First Read Paraphrase

When you **paraphrase**, you retell what you have read in your own words. Technical texts often contain new and unfamiliar information. You need to reread carefully and think about what you have read. Then try to explain this complex information in your own words. For example, you might restate the sentence "The caterpillar gets bigger through molts in which it sheds its skin" as "Each time a caterpillar sheds its skin, it gets bigger."

Paraphrasing is different from summarizing because summarizing only includes the main idea and important details. When you paraphrase, you don't have to worry about length as long as you retell the text in your own words. Here are some tips to help you paraphrase. First, read the selection carefully. Then, read it again and look for words or phrases that you don't understand. When you think you understand those words or phrases, say or write your ideas in your own words.

Try It Read this paragraph.

> Water striders are insects that live on the surface of a pond. They have little bunches of hair on the bottoms of their legs. The hairs trap air, and that helps to keep the insect from sinking.

 Discuss **Now try to paraphrase what you have read. Retell the paragraph in your own words.**

As you read, record your answers about paraphrasing on the Close Reading Worksheet on page 253.

Practice the Skill

Authors use **text structures** to organize their writing. One text structure is called problem and solution. A **problem** is an issue, and a **solution** is what is used or done to solve that problem. An author might state a problem and then provide possible solutions or discuss several problems and the ways that each has been solved. For example, an author might write an article about the pollution caused by plastic bottles and include some solutions for how to avoid this.

When you read problem-and-solution texts, watch how the author organizes the writing. Look for problems. Then find how the problems were solved. Often the writer will use the words *problem* and *solution* in the text, and you can use these words as clues.

Try It Read these paragraphs.

> Some apartment dwellers have a problem—they're not allowed to have a dog. If they love dogs, they can try being a dog sitter. This way, they can have dogs to love, just not to live with.
>
> But what if the people don't know anybody with dogs? They may need to advertise in order to get customers. They could put up a flyer at a pet store or post an ad on an Internet job board.

Discuss **What problems are discussed in these paragraphs? Circle the problems. Now look for the ways that the problems can be solved. Underline the solutions.**

As you read, complete the Problem-and-Solution Chart on page 254.

Try Eating in Space

Reread the third and fourth sentences in paragraph 2. Paraphrase the sentences in your own words.

Why was John Glenn given a tube of applesauce to eat on a space mission?

1   In 1962, John Glenn was the first U.S. astronaut to eat on a mission in **space**. His "meal" was applesauce squeezed from a tube. Since that time, astronauts have asked for meals like the ones they eat at home. They need energy to stay active and healthy while on a space mission. Since food is an important part of our lives, why shouldn't astronauts want good food when they're on a mission?

2   Scientists have had to figure out ways to make sure that astronauts get healthy, tasty meals in space. Spaceships don't have much storage space, and they don't carry refrigerators. Also, astronauts live in a low-gravity environment on a spaceship. Gravity is the natural force that causes things to fall toward Earth. In space, the pull of gravity is less than it is on Earth, so people and objects float up and are suspended in space. This creates all kinds of problems for eating in space.

Storage and Safety

3   Spaceships don't have many cabinets to store food, like home kitchens do. Instead, they have small areas for storing food. Scientists had to find ways to prepare foods that would fit into these small areas. They achieved this by making individual food packages and sending up just enough for the expected length of a mission. Enough food is sent for two additional days, in case missions are extended due to bad weather on Earth, which would make reentry dangerous.

4   Astronauts can't take out the trash, which means that they have to store trash in the spaceship. To do this, they use machines to **compact** the trash bags. These machines press and squeeze bags of trash until they are much smaller.

5   Since spaceships may not have refrigerators, scientists prepare foods in ways that make them safe to store and eat without refrigeration. One way they do this is to dehydrate, or remove the water, from foods before they are packaged. The dryness prevents the growth of bacteria. These foods are stabilized and will remain safe even without refrigeration. Astronauts add water before they eat or drink the foods. Juices, soups, eggs, and cereals are prepared this way.

6   Another way to prepare food is to cook the foods first on Earth and then put the cooked foods into cans. Astronauts can just open the cans and eat foods like tuna fish and fruit. Other foods, such as beef stew and soups, are heated in a warming oven.

Paraphrase the second and third sentences in paragraph 5.

In paragraph 5, the author describes a problem—no refrigeration. What solutions does the author give? Write the solutions on the **Problem-and-Solution Chart**.

Dehydrated food

It's All about Taste

Salt and pepper cause problems for astronauts in space. How have scientists solved the problem? Write the solution on the **Problem-and-Solution Chart**.

7   Many astronauts say that foods often taste different in space. The experience of being in low gravity may affect senses such as taste and smell. Astronauts add hot sauce and other spicy seasonings to their food. These seasonings give their food an extra kick!

8   Salt and pepper can make food taste better, but it's not easy to use these items in space. On Earth, people can **shake** salt or pepper on food, and it lands on the food. But when astronauts shake salt or pepper, it flies into the air. Pepper up the nose can make astronauts sneeze. Flying salt can damage the equipment. Scientists discovered a way to prevent this from happening. They mix salt with water, and they combine pepper with oil. Then they put the liquids into bottles. Astronauts use droppers to put salt and pepper into their food instead of shaking it.

9   Astronauts have favorite foods, and they want these foods when on a space mission. Scientists at NASA will ask the astronauts for their favorite food choices. Then they prepare the foods and have the astronauts sample them. The astronauts taste and rate each type of food. A score of 1 means "no good," but a score of 9 means "we love it." Only foods that get a score of 6 or higher will be part of the astronauts' menus.

NASA stands for National Aeronautics and Space Administration. This government agency is responsible for space exploration and research.

Hold Onto Your Seat . . . and Your Fork!

10   Low gravity is the reason why silverware will float off a table and into space. Scientists have developed methods for preventing this from happening. They have designed special food trays that contain straps, magnets, and fabric fasteners. The straps go around an astronaut's lap and hold the tray in place. Magnets hold forks, knives, spoons, and scissors, which the astronauts use to open food packages. The fabric fasteners hold food containers onto the tray.

11   Astronauts also learn to hold and eat foods carefully, so they don't fly off a plate into space. An astronaut will cut small openings in food packages. Then he or she holds the package close to his or her mouth so that the food doesn't have to travel far. Eating scrambled eggs in space requires careful concentration!

12   Some types of foods crumble, such as bread and crackers. The crumbs they form float away in low gravity. Astronauts have discovered that tortillas work much better than bread. They can spread peanut butter and jelly on a tortilla and make a tasty PB and J. Or they can put rice, beans, and cheese in a tortilla and roll it up to make a meal in a wrap.

In paragraph 10, you learn that silverware floats in space. What have scientists done to solve this problem? Write the solution on the **Problem-and-Solution Chart**.

How do tortillas help solve the problem of crumbs in space?

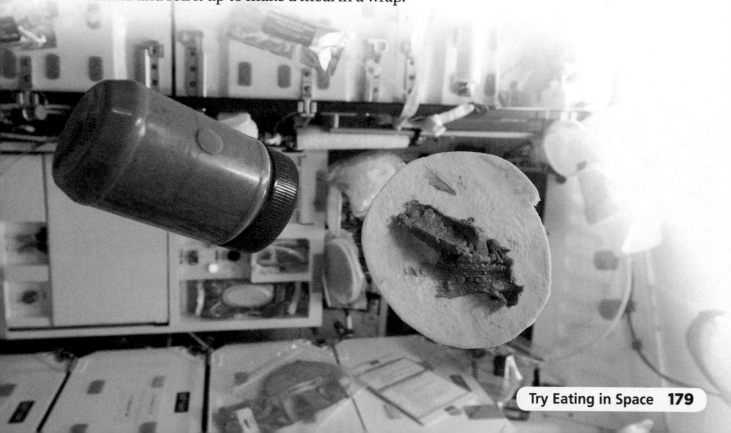

Cooking on the International Space Station

Paraphrase the last two sentences of the article. ✏️

How does Sandra Magnus solve the problem of foods and cooking tools floating into space? Write your answer on the **Problem-and-Solution Chart**.

Apply

Based on what you learned about eating in a low-gravity environment, what other activities would be difficult to do while in space? Explain. ✏️

13   In 2000, astronauts began traveling to the International Space Station (ISS). The ISS is a laboratory in space where astronauts from around the world live and work. One astronaut, Sandra Magnus, has tried cooking on the space station. This activity is nothing like cooking on Earth. In a kitchen here, chefs and other people put foods, seasonings, and tools on a **counter** and start cooking. You can probably imagine what happens to these items in the low-gravity environment of the space station.

14   Magnus solved the problem of floating foods and tools by using duct tape. This type of tape is strong, sticky, and waterproof. Magnus puts strips of duct tape on the counter and places tools on top of them. The tape keeps her food and tools from floating away. She also places pieces of trash on a strip of tape, rolls it up, and puts it in the trash bag.

15   Magnus uses another handy tool—plastic bags—when she cooks. She puts all of her ingredients into a plastic bag. Then she places the bag on a strip of duct tape and mashes items while they are inside the bag. She also uses a plastic bag as a bowl and uses her hand to mix ingredients inside it.

16   Scientists have discovered smart ways to prepare, package, and cook healthy, tasty foods for astronauts. They are continuing to experiment with food, such as growing hydroponic vegetables in space—a way to grow produce without soil. This is one way to ensure astronauts will be able to eat nutritious meals far from home.

Sandra Magnus cooking aboard the International Space Station

Vocabulary: Context Clues and Multiple-Meaning Words

Context clues are words near an unfamiliar word that give hints to its meaning. These words may be in the same sentence as the unfamiliar word or in surrounding sentences. Some words in English have more than one meaning. They are called **multiple-meaning words**. You must use context clues to figure out which meaning is intended.

Try It Read this sentence from "Try Eating in Space."

> In 1962, John Glenn was the first U.S. astronaut to eat on a mission in **space**.

The word *space* has more than one meaning. Underline the context clues that help you figure out the correct meaning.

Discuss ⟩ **Brainstorm different meanings of the word *space*.**

Find the following multiple-meaning words in the article. Look for the context clues that help you understand what each word means. Then write a definition for each word, and use it in a sentence.

1. **compact,** p. 177 _____

_____

2. **shake,** p. 178 _____

_____

3. **counter,** p. 180 _____

_____

Respond to Text: Text Structure: Problem and Solution

"Trapped!" discusses how scientists have come up with a procedure for rescuing whales that have been trapped in fishing lines. Scientists continue to face challenging problems in carrying out this procedure.

Try It Think about what you learned about problems and solutions from reading this technical text.

 Discuss **What problems are discussed in "Trapped!"? Which one do you think is the most challenging? How successful have scientists been in solving this problem? Your responses should be based on evidence from the text.**

On Your Own State the problem that you think is the most challenging to solve, and tell why. Then explain how scientists have used knowledge and creativity to solve the problem. Include facts and details from the text in your explanation. Use the next page to help you plan your response. Then write your paragraph on a separate sheet of paper.

Checklist for a Good Response

A good paragraph

✔ states the problem you think is the most challenging.

✔ explains why you think this is the most challenging problem.

✔ describes how scientists have creatively solved the problem.

✔ includes facts and details from the text.

✔ shows your understanding of the problem and solutions.

✔ includes a topic sentence, supporting ideas, and a concluding sentence.

My Review of Problem and Solution Text Structure

1. **Topic Sentence** I think the problem of _____

    _____ has been the most challenging one to solve because

    _____ .

2. **Detail Sentences** The sentences of your paragraph should include facts and details that explain how scientists have solved this problem. Use this chart to organize your ideas.

Problem	Solutions
Scientists have developed several ways to try to solve this problem.	Some of the solutions include: • • •

3. **Concluding Sentence** Your final sentence should sum up details and show how scientists have creatively solved this problem.

    _____

    _____

    _____

    On a separate sheet of paper, write your paragraph.

Read on Your Own

Read the article independently three times, using the skills you have learned. Then answer the Comprehension Check questions.

First Read Practice the first-read skills you learned in this lesson.

Second Read Practice the second-read skills you learned in this lesson.

Third Read Think critically about the article.

Curling: The Roaring Game

1 If you were asked to list the winter sports you know, you would probably include skiing, skating, and ice hockey. You may have played these sports or watched them on television. You probably wouldn't include the sport of curling. But curling is also a winter sport. Like hockey, curling is played on ice. It has become so popular that it is now an Olympic sport. Still, many people do not know much about curling.

Paraphrase Reread the last sentence in paragraph 2. Think about how you would retell the information in your own words.

2 The goal of curling is to slide a large stone down the ice into a circle-shaped target. The team that gets its stone closest to the center of the circle scores a point. Curling has been called the "roaring game" because the stone makes a roaring sound as it slides along the ice.

3 Curling was first played in the 1500s, when players got together and threw stones over a frozen pond. Today, curlers slide special stones with handles over an ice surface and use equipment called brooms to help move the stones. Curling has **developed** into a real sport.

In 1998, curling became an official sport in the Winter Olympics.

The Curling Surface

4   A curling **match** is played on a sheet of ice that is about 146 feet long and 14 feet wide. This is called the curling surface, or sheet. At each end of the surface is a goal, or target, called the house. In the center of each house is a small circle called the tee. Players try to slide each stone as close to the tee as they can.

5   A hack is a ledge frozen into the ice behind each house. Players put one foot on the hack and push off with the other foot. Hog lines are boundaries drawn across the ice surface in front of each house. Stones must slide over the hog lines in order to stay in play.

6   The ice for a curling match is colder than the ice used for a hockey game because this keeps the surface hard. If the ice isn't hard enough, it can cause a problem. When the stones hit the ice, they might make holes in it. Holes in the surface can affect how the stones move on the ice. Also, before every curling match, someone sprays the ice with tiny drops of water. When the drops freeze, they form tiny pebbles on the ice. This type of surface helps the stones move.

Main Idea and Details Think about the main idea in paragraph 6. Then think about the details that support the main idea.

Diagrams What is the target on a curling surface called? Circle the label. Then circle the label for the center of the target. The first one has been done for you.

Text Structure Think about a problem that might affect a curling match and how the problem has been addressed.

Diagram of a Curling Surface

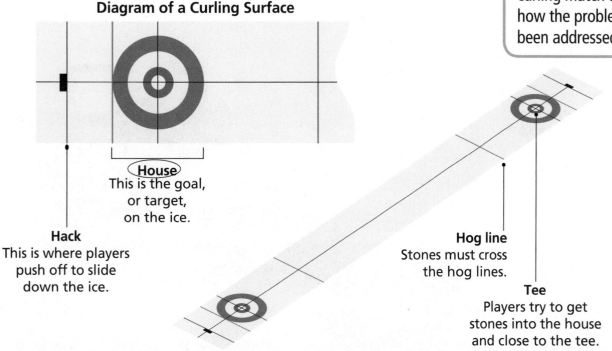

House
This is the goal, or target, on the ice.

Hack
This is where players push off to slide down the ice.

Hog line
Stones must cross the hog lines.

Tee
Players try to get stones into the house and close to the tee.

7   Two teams of four players each take part in a curling match. Each player plays one of four positions: lead, second, third, and skip. The skip is also the captain and best player of the team. This player decides on the team's plan and points out where players should try to place their stones. The lead is the first player to throw stones for his or her team. After the lead throws, the other players throw in this order: second, third, skip.

8   Players on a curling team wear special shoes that help them move. One shoe has a slider on the sole, which helps the players slide easily when they are sweeping, or brushing the ice to make it smooth. The other shoe has a piece that grips the ice, which holds players up and keeps them from falling.

9   Stones and brooms are the basic equipment used in a curling match. Curling stones are made of a type of rock known as granite. The stones are round and curved in on the bottom. This part is called the cup. Players use a handle on top of the stones to pick them up and throw them. The stones are made in several different colors. The brooms look like regular brooms but can have different types of brushes. The brushes are made of animal hair or human-made threads that are like hair.

Curling stones are made of polished granite so they slide easily across the ice.

How the Game Is Played

10   A curling match is made up of ten periods called ends. Here's how a match works. First, the lead player on a team throws a stone down the ice toward the house. Next, two other players slide down the ice ahead of the stone and use brooms to sweep the ice. This action helps the stone move faster over the ice. Players leave the stone where it stops.

11   Then, the lead player throws a second stone and repeats the activity. When he or she finishes, the lead player on the other team takes a turn and throws two stones. The player whose stone is closest to the tee wins and gets a point. Since each team throws eight stones, a team can score as many as eight points in an end. Players continue taking turns until each player on a team has the chance to throw two stones.

12   The players then begin to play the next end. This time they throw stones toward the other house. The team with the most points after ten ends wins the match. If there is a tie score, the teams play another end to break the tie.

Sequence Underline the words that give clues about the sequence of events in a curling end.

Critical Thinking Think about what skills you need to be a curler.

Players use the broom to sweep the ice and to help them keep their balance. Some players use the broom to point out where a teammate should aim the stone.

The Olympics and More!

Bar Graphs What does the bar graph below show? How many times has the U.S. men's team won? Draw a box around the information in the graph and the text.

Critical Thinking Think about the qualities of curling that make it an exciting game to play and to watch.

13   Today, curling is played in many places around the world. Children, teens, and adults play on teams at ice rinks. Curling clubs invite new members to come and learn what the sport is all about. They want people to have fun so that they'll want to come back and play. Experienced curlers teach newcomers how to move quickly and safely on the ice surface, how to balance as they slide, and how to brush the ice effectively.

14   Many countries have teams that are good enough to play in championship matches. One big event is the World Curling Championships. The best curling teams in the world play in this event every year. The U.S. men's team has won this event four times, and the U.S. women's team has won three times.

15   The best teams in the world can now compete in the Olympics. This wasn't always the case. Back in 1924, men's teams did play curling matches in the Olympics. But after that, curling was played just for show in the Olympics. Finally, in 1998, curling became an official Olympic sport again. Since that time, both men's and women's teams compete.

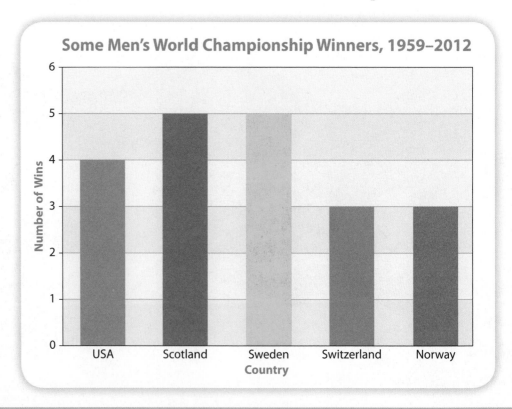

Some Men's World Championship Winners, 1959–2012

✔ Comprehension Check

1. What is the main idea of the section "How the Game Is Played"? What details support this main idea?

_____

_____

_____

_____

2. In your own words, describe a curling surface. Use information from the diagram and the text.

_____

_____

_____

_____

3. What has caused a problem in curling matches? Explain how this problem is now prevented.

_____

_____

_____

_____

4. Read this sentence from the article.

   A curling match is played on a sheet of ice that is about 146 feet long and 14 feet wide.

   What does the word *match* mean as it is used in this sentence?

   _____

   _____

5. Read this sentence from the article.

   Curling has developed into a real sport.

   Look up the word *developed* in a dictionary. Write the definition, and use the word in a sentence.

   _____

   _____

   _____

6. According to the bar graph, which men's teams have won the greatest number of World Curling Championship events?

   _____

   _____

Lesson 8

Literary Nonfiction:
Biography and Autobiography

A biography is the true story of a person's life as told by someone else. A writer must read about or talk to the subject in order to tell about the person's life in a new or different way.

An autobiography is the true story of a person's life as told by that person. For an autobiography, the writer chooses the most interesting events from his or her life and describes them in a way that no one else can. Look at this photo of President Barack Obama. What time in his life might he want to write about in his autobiography?

Skills Focus

Abraham Lincoln: A Biography

Draw Inferences   **Time Lines**

Rebecca Fire Fox: A Sculptor of Wood

Biography vs. Autobiography

Text Structure

Practice the Skill

First Read Draw Inferences

An **inference** is an educated guess about a text based on information from the author and your own prior knowledge. For example, a biography of President Barack Obama might not tell about all of his experiences in school. However, you know that presidents have to know a lot about the world and how it works. So, you can draw the inference that President Obama worked hard and got good grades in school.

Try It Read this paragraph from a biography.

> Helen Keller lost her ability to see and hear after an illness when she was a baby. This meant that she could not learn to speak or read. In her autobiography, she described her early years as a time of wildness and darkness. She often had temper tantrums.

Discuss What inference can you make about how Helen Keller felt as a child?

Read on to learn more about Helen Keller.

> When Keller was six years old, her life changed when she met teacher Annie Sullivan. Sullivan taught Keller sign language so the girl could express her needs. Once Keller learned a few basic words, she burned to know the names for everything around her. She no longer viewed the world as a dark prison but as a place of endless possibilities.

Discuss Based on this information, what can you infer about Helen Keller's experiences? What evidence in the text supports this? Underline the evidence.

As you read, complete the Inferences Chart on page 255.

Practice the Skill

Second Read Time Lines

A **time line** is a graphic that shows a series of related events and tells the dates when they took place. A time line is organized in time order, or chronological order, so you can see which event came first and which events followed it. Like most graphics, a time line presents information clearly and simply. It has a title and clear labels that help you read it.

Try It Look at this time line.

Some Events of World War II

1939

September 1, 1939
Word War II begins in Europe.

1941

December 7, 1941
Japan attacks the United States at Pearl Harbor.

June 6, 1944
U.S troops and allies invade France on D-day.

1944

1945

May 8, 1945
Germany surrenders.

August 14, 1945
Japan surrenders.

Discuss **What years are included in this time line? What happened in 1941? Circle the event.**

As you read, record your answers to questions about time lines on the Close Reading Worksheet on page 256.

Purpose for Reading

Read along with your teacher. Each time, read for a different purpose.

First Read   Focus on drawing inferences based on details in the text.

Second Read   Focus on understanding time lines.

Third Read   Focus on evaluating the text critically.

Abraham Lincoln:
A Biography

What detail supports the inference that education played an important role in Lincoln's life? Underline the detail. Then write it on the **Inferences Chart**.

1   Abraham Lincoln, the sixteenth president of the United States, was born in 1809 in a log cabin in rural Kentucky. His family was strict. They were also against slavery. In the 1800s, farmers in many states in our country used slaves to grow crops. Kentucky was one of them. Lincoln's family later moved to Indiana, a state that did not allow slavery.

2   In 1828, Lincoln visited New Orleans. Passing through the city, he came upon a slave **auction**. Lincoln had been taught that slavery was wrong. It upset him to see fellow human beings sold as objects to the highest bidders. He began to think more seriously about the issue.

How did holding so many different jobs help Lincoln to learn and grow?

3   Lincoln soon settled in New Salem, Illinois, where he worked as a surveyor, a shopkeeper, and a postmaster. Honesty was important to Lincoln. According to one story, he walked several miles to deliver change to a customer who had left too much money. To learn about the law and fairness, he read widely—history books, essays, newspapers, law books, the Bible, poetry, and the U.S. Constitution.

4   Lincoln entered the world of politics in 1832. Running for a seat in the state legislature, he rode his horse all over the county, giving speeches and meeting voters. He lost that first contest but discovered his love of traveling and public speaking. He won the next election in 1834.

5   When Lincoln took his seat in the state capitol, many people thought he was a comical sight. Tall and bony, Lincoln had to borrow money to buy a good suit. But he didn't care much about looks. He had sharpened his mind for the law and for politics. Now he had a chance to use these talents to help people and make a difference.

6   Lincoln soon became a successful lawyer as well as a **legislator**, or lawmaker. In 1839, he met Mary Todd, an intelligent and well-educated young woman from a well-off family. Mrs. Lincoln's wealth would help support the family and pay for her husband's political campaigns. They married in 1842 and had four sons: Robert, Edward, Willie, and Tad. In 1850, when Edward was only three years old, he became ill and died. Edward's unexpected death was a great blow to Lincoln, but it would not be the only sad event in the future president's life.

What inference can you make based on the detail that his son's death "would not be the only sad event in the future president's life"? Write the inference on the **Inferences Chart**.

Why might marrying an intelligent woman have been helpful to Lincoln's career as a politician?

Lincoln educated himself by reading books, but he also valued common sense. As a lawmaker and as president, he was wise but practical when making important decisions.

Abraham Lincoln: A Biography   195

What details support the inference that Lincoln's stand against slavery helped him become a candidate for president? Underline them and then write them on the **Inferences Chart.**

What event in Lincoln's early life appears in the time line but not in the text?

7   In 1854, Lincoln was attending a fair in Bloomington, Illinois, when he heard a political opponent giving a speech. Stephen Douglas was standing on a small stage and speaking out in favor of slavery. At this time, half the states in the country allowed slavery. Lincoln felt this man's words had to be challenged, so he asked to speak after him. The crowd listened carefully as Lincoln explained why slavery was wrong. When Lincoln called slavery "a gross outrage against the law of nature," everyone applauded.

8   Four years later, Lincoln ran against Stephen Douglas for a seat in the United States Senate. Lincoln lost the race, but his debates with Douglas made him famous. In 1860, when the Republican Party needed a candidate for president, they eventually chose the simple and humble man from the backwoods. Slavery would be the most important issue in the 1860 election, and Lincoln's strong feelings about the issue were well-known.

9   As the campaign went on, a number of southern states threatened to leave the Union if Lincoln were elected. On November 6, he was elected president. On December 20, South Carolina became the first state to **secede**, or withdraw, from the United States. The rest of the southern states would soon join South Carolina to form their own nation, the Confederate States of America. On April 12, 1861, the first shots of the Civil War were fired. The Confederacy and the United States were at war.

Abraham Lincoln's Life to 1860

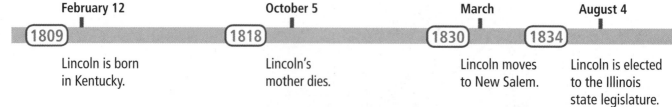

February 12	October 5	March	August 4
1809	1818	1830	1834
Lincoln is born in Kentucky.	Lincoln's mother dies.	Lincoln moves to New Salem.	Lincoln is elected to the Illinois state legislature.

10   President Lincoln was forced to send Union troops from the North to fight against the Confederate troops in the South. Both sides hoped the war would be won quickly. However, after the Confederacy won an important battle, it was clear the Civil War would be a long fight. The president felt deeply sad about the loss of life on both sides, but he was determined to bring the states back together.

11   During the war, President and Mrs. Lincoln experienced another terrible loss to their family. Their third son, Willie, became ill and died in 1862, when he was eleven years old. Around this time, deep lines began to form in Lincoln's cheeks and brow. His mood became sad as well.

12   Some people in the government told Lincoln to keep quiet about the issue of slavery, but the president thought differently. On January 1, 1863, he issued the Emancipation Proclamation. This was a brave thing to do. This official **document** granted freedom to people who were enslaved in the Confederate areas still in rebellion. For Lincoln, the war now had a clear goal: it would not only bring the states back together, but it would also end slavery in this country forever.

What details support the inference that Lincoln wanted to free enslaved people? Write the details from the text on the **Inferences Chart**.

How many times did Lincoln meet with Douglas for a debate? Circle the answer in the time line.

Why do you think some people in the government told Lincoln to keep quiet about the issue of slavery?

Civil War, 1862
- Union States
- Confederate States
- Border States
- Territories

For four long years, the Confederate states in the South were at war with the Union states in the North. President Lincoln's goal was to reunite the nation and to end slavery.

November 4
1842
Lincoln marries Mary Todd.

August–October
1858
Lincoln and Stephen Douglas participate in seven debates.

November 6
1860
Lincoln is elected president.

December 20
South Carolina leaves the United States.

Based on what you know about Lincoln, how do you think he felt about the end of the war? Write your inference and details from the text on the **Inferences Chart**.

Based on the text, what event is missing from the time line?

What information appears in the time line that does not appear in the text?

Judge

Was Lincoln a good president? Why or why not? Use evidence from the text to support your answer.

13   The war dragged on. After every battle, Lincoln asked for the news: Who had won? Who had lost? How many soldiers were killed? How much longer could the war go on? After each loss, he went to his generals to work on a better plan. In 1863, Union forces beat the Confederates in a key battle in Gettysburg, Pennsylvania. It was a turning point in the war. The Confederate army would never recover its strength. Still, the war continued with huge losses on both sides until April 9, 1865. On that day, Confederate general Robert E. Lee surrendered his forces. The war would soon be over.

14   Lincoln would not have long to enjoy the victory. On April 14, he attended a play at a theater in Washington, D.C., where a gunman stepped out of the shadows and shot him in the back of the head. It was a terrible wound, and within hours, Abraham Lincoln was dead. The nation began to mourn the loss of its leader.

15   Lincoln left an example of great leadership. He continued to inspire people long after his death. In 1963, almost a century after his death, people remembered him and his words as they marched in support of the rights of African American citizens. They gathered in huge crowds at the foot of a statue made in his honor and gave speeches in support of a truly united nation where everyone is treated equally under the law. Had Lincoln been alive to see it, no doubt he would have been proud.

Abraham Lincoln's Later Life

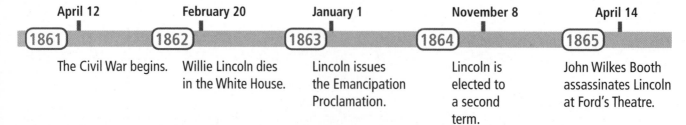

April 12	February 20	January 1	November 8	April 14
1861	**1862**	**1863**	**1864**	**1865**
The Civil War begins.	Willie Lincoln dies in the White House.	Lincoln issues the Emancipation Proclamation.	Lincoln is elected to a second term.	John Wilkes Booth assassinates Lincoln at Ford's Theatre.

Vocabulary: Context Clues

As you read, you will encounter new words that are unfamiliar or familiar words that are used in new ways. When that happens, look for context clues. **Context clues** are words or phrases that help you understand an unfamiliar word's meaning. They often appear in the same sentence as the word or in nearby sentences. After you use context clues to guess a word's meaning, double-check the definition in a dictionary.

Try It Read these sentences from "Abraham Lincoln: A Biography."

> Passing through the city, he came upon a slave **auction**. Lincoln had been taught that slavery was wrong. It upset him to see fellow human beings sold as objects to the highest bidders.

If you do not know what the word *auction* means, read the other words in the sentences. Identify the words that help you figure out the meaning of *auction*.

> Discuss **Brainstorm definitions of the word *auction*.**

The following words are found in "Abraham Lincoln: A Biography." Find the words and look for the context clues that help you understand what each word means. Then write a definition of the word.

1. **legislator**, p. 195 _____

_____

2. **secede**, p. 196 _____

_____

3. **document**, p. 197 _____

_____

Practice the Skill

A **biography** and an **autobiography** both tell the story of a person's life. As a reader, how can you tell them apart? The writer of an autobiography will use *I* to talk about himself or herself. But the writer of a biography will use *he* or *she* to refer to the subject. An autobiography often conveys the author's experiences in vivid detail and uses a style that sounds personal. A biography is more formal and includes information from other sources, such as letters, diaries, and interviews.

Try It   Read these paragraphs from a biography.

Billy Smalls had no idea as he walked onto the platform that he was beginning the longest unbroken streak of medal-winning dives in his sport's history. In an interview, he said he had "felt really calm" before his first dive.

His dive was so good that the judges took extra time to score it. "I thought I had messed up," Smalls said later. Then the scores glowed on the screen, and he knew he'd made history.

Now read this paragraph from the same subject's autobiography.

As I strode to the end of the board, a great confidence overwhelmed me. I went through my routine in my mind and then hurled myself off the board. After my dive, I kept calm until the judges' scores finally appeared. I knew they would be perfect.

> **Discuss**   **What differences do you see between the biography and autobiography? Does one seem to be more reliable? Why?**

As you read, record your answers to questions about biography and autobiography on the Close Reading Worksheet on page 257.

Practice the Skill

Text structure refers to the way a piece of writing presents information. Because biographies and autobiographies tell the story of a person's life, their authors usually use a text structure called **chronological order**, or time order. Most stories of a person's life start at the beginning and tell the events in the order that they happened. The author uses clue words such as *first*, *then*, *next*, *after*, *later*, and *finally* to tell when events took place.

Sometimes, stories start at the most exciting moment and then jump backward in time. Such a story might not return to the high point until the very end. Saving the details about what actually happened helps keep the reader interested and focused.

Try It Reread the excerpts from the biography and autobiography of Billy Smalls on page 200.

 What event do both accounts cover? Do both writers use chronological order? How do you know?

As you read the excerpts, put boxes around the clue words that help you follow the order of events. Also, think about when each story starts and why the author chose to start the story at that point.

As you read, complete the Chronology Chart on page 258.

Rebecca Fire Fox: A Sculptor of Wood

Is the selection a biography or an autobiography? Circle details in paragraph 1 that tell you.

Read "An Artist's Beginnings." How does Fire Fox first become interested in making things? Write your answer on the **Chronology Chart**.

Why do you think the story of Rebecca Fire Fox begins where it does?

This autobiography is a fictional work about a made-up person that models the characteristics and text features common in authentic texts of this type.

1   I stood at the podium holding the award in my shaking hands. I was feeling so grateful. This was the greatest honor of my life. But before I could accept it, I needed to explain why I was receiving an important prize after a single exhibition of my art. I wanted the audience to understand how my art was influenced by my life as a Lakota Indian. As I began to speak, I thought of all the times I'd **wandered** aimlessly in the woods, looking for the perfect piece of wood to carve.

An Artist's Beginnings

2   My earliest memory is of taking apart my father's handheld radio when I was five years old. All I learned was how to make the thing stop working. But the shapes of the parts **fascinated** me. There was a tiny cone of tin and coils of copper wire. I loved how they fit together perfectly. The idea that someone could make something so interesting was exciting to me. I had no metal cones and coils, but I could make art out of the things I found around me.

3 By age seven, I was building things out of what we now call *found objects*. I saw them—used ice-cream sticks and soda straws—in the trash or on the ground outside the local grocery store. No one else wanted them, but I used them to build unusual shapes and structures. I spent hours twisting, bending, and gluing them together.

4 My family didn't understand my love of building things from garbage, and they certainly never displayed my art on the refrigerator. The Fire Foxes were traditional. They worked with wool and dye to create rugs so beautiful that many were later sold to museums and hung on walls. My family had made the rugs for people to put on their floors and walk over, but most people just wanted to admire them. My family believed hard work was good, play was bad, and making something just to look at was a waste of effort. Where did I fit in? Perhaps it was this attitude that drove me into the woods near our home. What I found there would change the rest of my life.

Are the events in Fire Fox's life told in chronological order? Draw a box around the clue that tells you. Enter the next event in her life on the **Chronology Chart**.

How did Fire Fox feel as an artistic child in a family that did not fully appreciate art?

Lakota rug

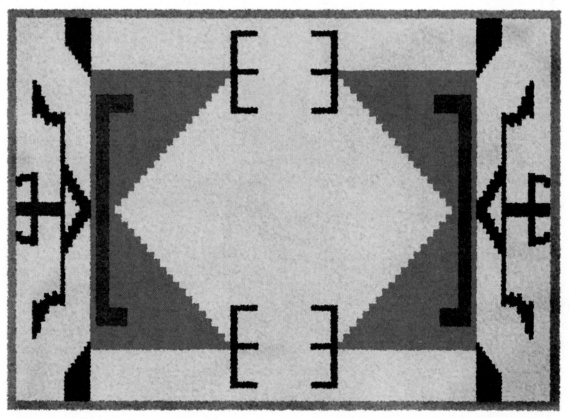

My First Sculpture

The author wants to make her writing personal, so she includes interesting details about her life. What two details reveal something about the author? Circle them.

5   I had just turned twelve years old, and as I wandered among some fallen tree limbs, all thoughts of ice-cream sticks and soda straws disappeared from my head. I knelt beside a branch. The wood was blond with darker rings and edged in black where lightning had struck it. The rings formed beautiful shapes. I wanted to cut into the wood and carve it to make shapes that had never been seen before.

What age is the author in this section? Draw a box around the word that tells you. What happens to her at this age? Write your answer on the **Chronology Chart**.

6   I started small. First, I took out my pocketknife and cut into a chunk of wood about the size of my hand. I gently shaved away the wood to create a new shape. In the end, the piece looked like a rough lump, but I was pleased.

7   Over time, I learned how to carve wood well, and my art got better and better. As I got older, I'd lie awake in my bed and **envision** the shape I wanted the wood to take.

The artist used woodworking tools such as these to create her wood carvings.

Next Stop: Getting an Education

8   By age fourteen, I knew what I wanted: to become so skilled with the tools and materials that I could make beautiful artwork. But in my high school woodshop class, I would not learn how to work with special cutting tools like an adze or a Japanese saw. No, the route to what I needed would have to be unique, especially for a Lakota born on the reservation.

9   As I considered my choices for schooling, I learned that I was lucky to be a Native American teenager in 1975. The 1970s was a time when Native Americans were beginning to stand up for their rights as citizens. For the first time, other Americans became aware of how poorly Native Americans had been treated. As a result, the government had started a scholarship program for Native Americans who wanted to study at schools far from their reservations. I got a grant that helped pay for a trip to study in Japan.

10   My teacher there, Mr. Saitou, encouraged me to think big. "Nothing is impossible," he used to say. He understood that I wasn't trying to **astound** others with my art. I simply wanted to carve a material that came alive in my hands. Mr. Saitou talked a lot about respecting the spirit of trees. This wasn't hard for me—not just because I'm Native American and I feel these things in my heart. I had always talked to the wood as I carved. I'd ask, "What shape are you trying to be?" "How can I reveal your inner beauty?" I spent three years studying in Japan and learning to carve wood. Then it was time to go home.

What details on this page reveal the author's inner thoughts?

What life events are described on this page? Enter them on the **Chronology Chart**.

Why do you think the author shares the details of her people's history with readers?

What important events happen on this page? Enter the events on the **Chronology Chart**.

Analyze

Do you think Rebecca Fire Fox would be just as proud of her accomplishments if she had not won the award? Why or why not? Use evidence from the text to support your answer.

11   I returned home at age seventeen and faced the challenge of how to be an American artist. At first I had trouble fitting in. My family and friends said I had changed. It's true. I liked to drink tea, and I would sometimes use a Japanese word instead of an English one. I had trouble speaking with people, but the wood in the forest still spoke to me. It told me to tell the story of my people.

12   So, I began to make carvings that represent the history of the Lakota. I lovingly sculpted the symbols that are important to us—the buffalo that once roamed our lands and the horses we used to ride on the plains. I shaped the faces of the explorers Lewis and Clark, whom we encountered peacefully in 1804, and the white settlers who came afterward in their wagons. I cried as I carved images of the war with the white soldiers, which ended terribly in 1877 when we were placed on reservations. Each of my hundred sculptures expressed pride in my people and history.

13   Later, at age twenty, when I accepted an award for my achievement in art, I was overwhelmed. I still have so much more to do with my art. As long as the wood continues to speak to me, I will carve it and be surprised and delighted by what emerges from it.

As a young child, the artist wandered among the trees of the Black Hills, in South Dakota, in search of inspiration.

Vocabulary: Choose Precise Words

The ability to choose words that precisely convey an idea is an important skill. You can use a thesaurus, which lists synonyms, to help you find the right word. You can use a dictionary to check the meaning.

Try It Read this sentence from "Rebecca Fire Fox: A Sculptor of Wood."

As I began to speak, I thought of all the times I'd **wandered** aimlessly in the woods, looking for the perfect piece of wood to carve.

How does the word *wandered* affect the meaning of the sentence? What if a word with a similar meaning—such as *walked* or *strolled*—had been used instead?

> Discuss **How can replacing one word change the meaning?**

In the following sentences, explain how the author's word choice conveys the meaning precisely.

1. But the shapes of the parts **fascinated** me. p. 202 _____

_____

2. As I got older, I'd lie awake in my bed and **envision** the shape I

wanted the wood to take. p. 204 _____

_____

3. He understood that I wasn't trying to **astound** others with my art.

p. 205 _____

Respond to Text: Draw Inferences

In "Abraham Lincoln: A Biography," you read a version of the great man's life. The selection told events in chronological order and focused on Lincoln's efforts to end slavery and unite the nation. Many Americans consider President Lincoln to be a hero, and many novels, plays, poems, films, and other biographies have been written about him. Based on these facts, what qualities can you infer are important to these Americans?

Try It Think about what you learned about drawing inferences.

> **Discuss** **What challenges did Lincoln face during his life? What were his special talents? Why did people admire him in his day? Use your discussion of these questions to draw inferences about the qualities he had that people still admire and consider heroic today.**

On Your Own Write a paragraph that explains why Lincoln remains a subject of great interest. Include details and evidence from "Abraham Lincoln: A Biography" to support your points. Use the next page to help you plan your response. Then write your paragraph on a separate sheet of paper.

Checklist for a Good Response

A good paragraph

✔ clearly states a main idea in the topic sentence.

✔ provides details and evidence that support these points.

✔ shows your understanding of what you have read.

✔ expresses your own point of view.

✔ ends with a concluding statement that sums up the paragraph.

My Inferences about Lincoln's Qualities

1. **Topic Sentence** Include this information in your first sentence:

    Based on "Abraham Lincoln: A Biography," I infer that people still

    admire Lincoln's qualities of _____ .

2. **Detail Sentences** The sentences of your paragraph should provide
    details that explain your inferences. Use this chart to organize your
    ideas and supporting details.

Inferences	Supporting Details from the Text or My Own Knowledge

3. **Concluding Sentence** Your final sentence should restate your
    conclusions with a new twist.

    _____

    _____

On a separate sheet of paper, write your paragraph.

Read on Your Own

Read the selection independently three times, using the skills you have learned. Then answer the Comprehension Check questions.

(**First Read**) Practice the first-read skills you learned in this lesson.

(**Second Read**) Practice the second-read skills you learned in this lesson.

(**Third Read**) Think critically about the selection.

Gertrude Ederle: Queen of the Waves

Draw Inferences
Think about the inference you can draw about Gertrude Ederle's strength and talents, based on the details on this page.

Biography vs. Autobiography
Think about how the language of the passage would be different if it were an autobiography. Think about how Ederle might tell the story in her own words.

1   Gertrude Ederle was the first great American female swimmer. She was born in New York City in 1905. Her parents took her and their other children to swim at the local pool. They also went on summer vacations to the New Jersey shore, where Ederle first learned to dodge the ocean waves. Her interest in swimming grew. As a teen, she left school to compete as a member of the Women's Swimming Association. She won her first championship when she was sixteen. By the time she was twenty-one, Ederle held twenty-nine national and world swimming records. She seemed unstoppable in the water.

2   At the 1924 Olympics, Ederle stood on the podium to collect her third medal. She had done an amazing feat. First, she won a gold medal in the 4 × 100–meter relay. Then she won two bronze medals in the 100-meter and 400-meter freestyle events. These medals showed she was one of the best female swimmers in the world. Yet, Ederle had a greater goal. She wanted to be the first woman in the world to swim across the English Channel, a narrow body of water that separates the countries of England and France. Many men had tried to achieve this, but only five had succeeded. Could Ederle do it?

Why Ederle's Goal Seemed Impossible

3   Ederle's idea was nearly unthinkable in her day. To understand why, you need to know a little about the world in which she lived. In the 1920s, women had only recently won the right to vote. Only 20 percent of American women worked outside the home, and few were serious athletes. This was because many people in society thought that winning at sports was unladylike.

4   Another challenge was the English Channel itself. It was—and still is—difficult and dangerous to swim. At its narrowest point, the Channel is only twenty-one miles wide. <u>But the water is extremely cold at all times of year.</u> Then there is the constant pounding of the waves from the west. They cause currents that force swimmers off course, so they have to swim longer and farther, which is tiring. Plus, the water is filled with jellyfish, which give a painful and irritating sting.

5   In 1925, Ederle traveled to France to make her first attempt to swim across the Channel. She failed after spending 8 hours and 43 minutes in the water. Other people might have given up, but Ederle would not. Swimming was her life, and nothing could change that. Also, she liked to win.

Draw Inferences
<u>Underline</u> details that support the inference that people in the 1920s probably did not think a woman was strong enough to swim the English Channel. The first one has been done for you.

Critical Thinking
Think about what it means to be the first person to complete an amazing feat.

Gertrude Ederle was a natural-born swimmer who competed at the highest levels long before many women were involved in sports.

Ederle Does the Impossible

Text Structure Think about the order in which the events are told. Consider what happens first, next, and last.

6   In 1926, Ederle returned to France with her family and her trainer. On August 6 of that year, she made a second attempt to swim across the English Channel. Ederle wore only a two-piece swimsuit and a bathing cap. She covered her body with **lanolin**. The thick, greasy lotion would help keep her warm and prevent jellyfish stings.

Text Structure (Circle) the sentence that tells what Ederle accomplished in 1926.

7   For hours, Ederle stroked her way through the cold, gray water as her family and trainer followed behind in a tugboat. After 14 hours and 31 minutes, Ederle reached the English shore. She was the first woman to cross the English Channel, and she had beaten the men's record by 1 hour and 59 minutes. Ederle's record would stand unbroken for twenty-four years. She considered it her greatest achievement.

Critical Thinking Think about why Ederle's achievement was considered so significant.

8   So did many others. When Ederle returned home to New York, crowds of fans stood at the harbor to greet her boat. They were thrilled that one of their own—an American, a New Yorker, a woman—had done the impossible. They gave her a hero's welcome and a ticker tape parade. Ederle rode through the streets of New York while tons of shredded paper were tossed from windows in the skyscrapers above. The people cheered. At City Hall, crowds **mobbed** her as Mayor Jimmy Walker offered his congratulations.

Ederle was covered with lanolin for the swim.

Events in Gertrude Ederle's Early Life

October 23
1905
Born in New York City

Summer
1921
Wins her first swimming championship

9   A sports writer at the *New York Herald* newspaper, W.W. McGeehan, was not surprised by Ederle's successful swim. He described her has having "the bravest pair of eyes that ever looked into a face" and called her achievement "the greatest sports story in the world."

10   Ederle gained national attention, too. She visited President Calvin Coolidge at the White House in Washington, D.C. He hailed Ederle as "America's best girl."

After the English Channel

11   Gertrude Ederle had done what she had set out to do, but in 1926, she was still a young woman with a long life and career ahead of her. What could she do next? There were not a lot of choices, so Ederle became a professional swimmer and performer. She traveled around the country with a group of entertainers to demonstrate her swimming skills for paying audiences. Later, she even took part in a film about her life. However, her swimming career came to a sudden end in 1933, when she suffered a back injury. She went into retirement— at age twenty-eight. In 1939, she returned to the pool to perform in the Aquacade attraction at the New York World's Fair. After that, she stopped swimming professionally.

Time Lines (Circle) the event on the time line that happened right before Ederle's first attempt to swim the English Channel.

Text Structure (Circle) the words in paragraph 11 that help to show the order of events.

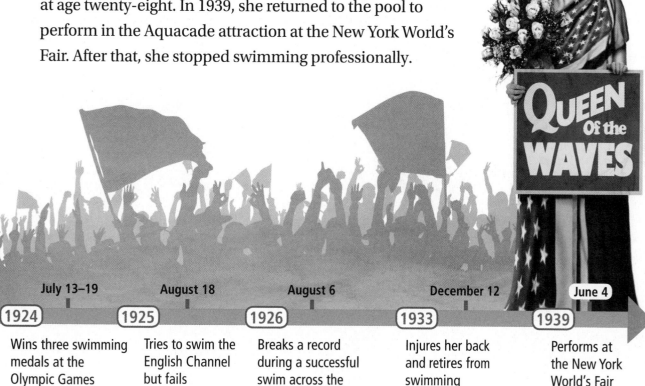

July 13–19	August 18	August 6	December 12	June 4
1924	**1925**	**1926**	**1933**	**1939**
Wins three swimming medals at the Olympic Games	Tries to swim the English Channel but fails	Breaks a record during a successful swim across the English Channel	Injures her back and retires from swimming	Performs at the New York World's Fair

You're Never Too Old to Swim

Draw Inferences
Think about what you can infer about Ederle's values, based on what she did with her later life.

12   Long after Ederle ended her career as a swimmer, she inspired others. When she lost her hearing in the 1940s, she began teaching deaf children to swim at a local pool. Many young women followed in her footsteps. In 1951, the American Florence May Chadwick became the first woman to swim the English Channel *twice*. Only a fraction of the swimmers who set out to cross the Channel actually makes it to the other side, but people still keep trying.

Text Structure What honors did Ederle receive later in her life? Circle them.

13   Later, Ederle received many honors. In 1965, she was inducted into the International Swimming Hall of Fame. Fifteen years later, she was invited into the International Women's Sports Hall of Fame.

14   Gertrude Ederle died in 2003 at the age of ninety-eight. Today, the Gertrude Ederle Recreation Center stands in a neighborhood in New York City close to where she grew up and learned to swim. It is a symbol of her remarkable life and athletic achievements. Of the seemingly impossible task of swimming the English Channel, Ederle once said this: "I just knew if it could be done, it had to be done, and I did it." For her, a record-breaking swim was just that simple.

The dotted red line on this map shows where Gertrude Ederle crossed the English Channel on August 6, 1926.

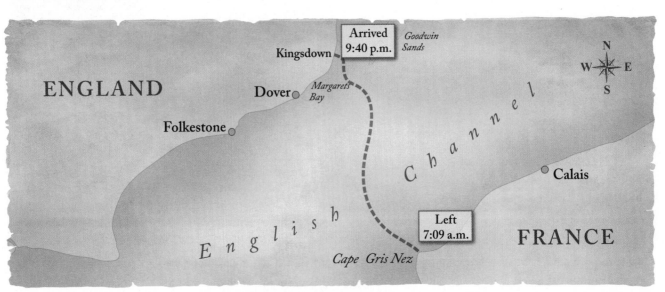

✅ Comprehension Check

1. What did Gertrude Ederle's decision to swim the English Channel say about the kind of person she was?

_____

_____

_____

_____

2. Does the author tell the events of Ederle's life in chronological order? How do you know?

_____

_____

_____

_____

3. Look at the time line on pages 212–213. During which years was Ederle swimming, winning medals, and breaking records?

_____

_____

_____

_____

4. Read this sentence from the biography.

   Ederle's record would stand unbroken for twenty-four years. She considered it her greatest achievement.

   How might this observation have been expressed differently in an autobiography?

   _____

   _____

   _____

   _____

5. Read these sentences from the biography.

   She covered her body with lanolin. The thick, greasy lotion would help keep her warm and prevent jellyfish stings.

   Circle the words that help you understand what *lanolin* is.

6. Read this sentence from the biography.

   At City Hall, crowds mobbed her as Mayor Jimmy Walker offered his congratulations.

   What does *mobbed* mean? How would the sentence have changed in meaning if another word had been used, such as *surrounded*?

   _____

   _____

   _____

Glossary

act a large section of a drama (Lesson 3)

adage a saying that expresses a truth about human nature (Lesson 2)

allusion a word or phrase that refers to a well-known story or event (Lesson 1)

antonyms words that mean the opposite of each other (Lesson 6)

autobiography the true story of a person's life as told by that person (Lesson 8)

bar graph a graphic that uses columns of different lengths to show and compare information (Lesson 7)

biography the true story of a person's life as told by someone else (Lesson 8)

caption brief text that gives more information about what is shown in a diagram or photo (Lesson 7)

cast of characters a list at the beginning of a play that names all the characters who will appear, with a brief description of each one (Lesson 3)

cause the reason something happens (Lesson 6)

characters the people, animals, or other creatures in a story (Lesson 1)

chronological order a text structure that describes events in time order or sequence (Lesson 8)

compare to tell how two things are similar (Lesson 1)

context clues words near an unfamiliar word that can help the reader figure out what that word means (Lessons 2, 7, 8)

contrast to tell how two things are different (Lesson 1)

diagram a drawing that shows the parts that make up something or how something works (Lesson 7)

dialogue the words that characters speak in a play or story (Lesson 3)

dictionary a reference book that lists words alphabetically with their meanings, pronunciations, and other information (Lessons 1, 5, 7)

drama a play that is written to be performed by actors on a stage (Lesson 3)

draw conclusions to use details from a text, as well as your own prior knowledge and experience, to form an opinion or make an overall decision about the text (Lessons 2, 6)

effect what happens as the result of a cause (Lesson 6)

evidence facts and data that support the reasons why something is true (Lesson 6)

figurative language language that does not mean exactly what it says; two examples are simile and metaphor (Lesson 4)

firsthand account a report written by a person who witnessed the events he or she describes (Lesson 5)

first-person point of view a point of view in which the narrator is a character in the story and uses the pronoun *I* (Lesson 2)

glossary an alphabetical list of difficult words or technical terms and their meanings, usually found at the end of a book (Lesson 7)

historical nonfiction writing that tells about real events and people from the past (Lesson 5)

history term a word or phrase that relates to a historical topic (Lesson 5)

idiom a phrase whose meaning is different from the individual words that make it up (Lesson 2)

inference an educated guess about a text, based on information provided by the author and the reader's own prior knowledge and experience (Lessons 2, 8)

label brief text that names a part of a diagram (Lesson 7)

main idea the most important idea in a passage; it tells what the passage is mostly about (Lessons 5, 7)

metaphor a comparison of two unlike things that does not use the words *like* or *as* (Lesson 4)

meter the pattern of strongly and weakly stressed syllables in a poem (Lesson 4)

motivation the reason why a character acts, thinks, and feels the way he or she does (Lesson 3)

multiple-meaning words words that have more than one meaning (Lessons 3, 7)

myths very old stories that were passed down orally and that tell how a people or culture came to be or explain how something in the world works (Lesson 1)

paraphrase to retell what you have read in your own words (Lesson 7)

plot the series of events that happen in a story (Lesson 1)

poem writing that expresses ideas and feelings using colorful descriptions and often rhyme (Lesson 4)

point of view the perspective from which a story is told (Lesson 2)

prediction a guess about what will happen in the future, based on information already provided in the story (Lesson 3)

prefix a group of letters added to the beginning of a root (Lesson 2)

problem an issue that needs to be resolved (Lesson 7)

proverb a saying that gives advice about how to live one's life (Lesson 2)

reason an explanation that tells why something is true (Lesson 6)

rhyme the repetition of ending sounds in words at the end of lines in a poem (Lesson 4)

rhythm a pattern, or "beat," in a poem created by stressed and unstressed syllables (Lesson 4)

root the main part of a word that carries its meaning (Lessons 1, 2, 3)

scene a small section of a drama (Lesson 3)

science term an important word or phrase in a scientific nonfiction article (Lesson 6)

scientific nonfiction writing that gives facts about a science topic (Lesson 6)

secondhand account an account written by a person who did not witness the events he or she describes (Lesson 5)

sequence the order in which things happen, in a series of events or steps in a process (Lesson 7)

setting the time and location in which a story or drama takes place (Lessons 1, 3)

short story a brief, made-up piece of fiction with characters, a setting, and a plot (Lesson 2)

simile a comparison of two unlike things that uses the words *like* or *as* (Lesson 4)

solution what is done or used to solve a problem (Lesson 7)

stage directions italicized words in a play that tell the actors how to move or speak (Lesson 3)

stanza a group of lines organized within a poem, usually separated by a blank line space (Lesson 4)

suffix a group of letters added to the end of a root (Lesson 3)

summarize to use your own words to briefly restate a text, including only the main ideas and most important details (Lessons 3, 5)

supporting details facts and information that tell more about the main idea of a passage (Lessons 5, 7)

synonyms words that have the same or similar meanings (Lesson 4)

technical texts writings about science or technology topics that explain why something happens or describe a process or procedure (Lesson 7)

technology term a word that is important to understanding a topic in a technical text (Lesson 7)

text structure the way an author organizes ideas and information in a text; two examples are cause and effect and chronological order (Lessons 6, 7, 8)

theme the central idea or message in a story or poem (Lessons 1, 4)

thesaurus a book of synonyms, or words with similar meanings, listed in alphabetical order (Lesson 1)

third-person point of view a point of view in which the narrator is someone outside the story and uses the pronouns *he* or *she* (Lesson 2)

time line a graphic that shows dates and events on a line or bar, organized in time order (Lesson 8)

verse short lines of poetry (Lesson 4)

visualize to picture something in your mind (Lesson 4)

Acknowledgments

Photo Credits 5, 133, 153, 154, 164, 168, 195, 204, 205 Shutterstock; 37, 61, 87, 130, 137, 138, 139, 144, 147, 148, 157, 172, 186, 187, 206 Thinkstock; 109, 121 Library of Congress; 113, 176, 177, 178, 179, 180 NASA; 115 San Francisco History Center, San Francisco Public Library; 123, 124, 191, 211 Wikimedia Commons.

Illustrations 8–12 Martina Peluso, Advocate Art Agency; 16–20, 99 France Brassard, Wendy Lynn & Co.; 24–28 Q2A; 32–33 Brent Campbell, Tugeau; 40–44 Gerald Kelley, Bright Agency; 49–52 Caroline Romanet, Advocate Art Agency; 57–58 Courtney A. Martin, Tugeau; 65–68 Scott Brooks, Wilkinson Studio, Inc.; 73–76 Nicole Wong; 80–81, 83, 84 Jamie Pogue, Bright Agency; 90–94 Melinda Beavers, Beehive Agency; 100 Monika Filipina, Advocate Art Agency; 104–106 Gabrielle Grimard, Painted Words, Inc.; 114 Rob Schuster; 129 Jared Osterhold, Wilkinson Studio Inc; 145–146, 159, 161–162, 185, 203, 213–214 Peter Bull Art Studio; 197 Joe Lemmonier.

Name: _____

✏️ Close Reading Worksheet

First Read: Determine the Theme (orange boxes)

Page 9: The author might be building toward a big idea of _____

_____

because _____.

Page 11: The conflict between Prometheus and Zeus suggests the message or

theme that _____

_____.

Page 12: The theme of the story is _____

_____.

Third Read: Critical Thinking (blue boxes)

Page 10: Prometheus (does / does not) do the right thing by disobeying Zeus

because _____

_____.

Page 11: By overcoming their fears and listening to Prometheus, humans gain

fire and show that they are _____

_____.

Connect—Page 12: The gift of fire from Prometheus helps humans farm by

_____

_____.

Name: _____

Character Web

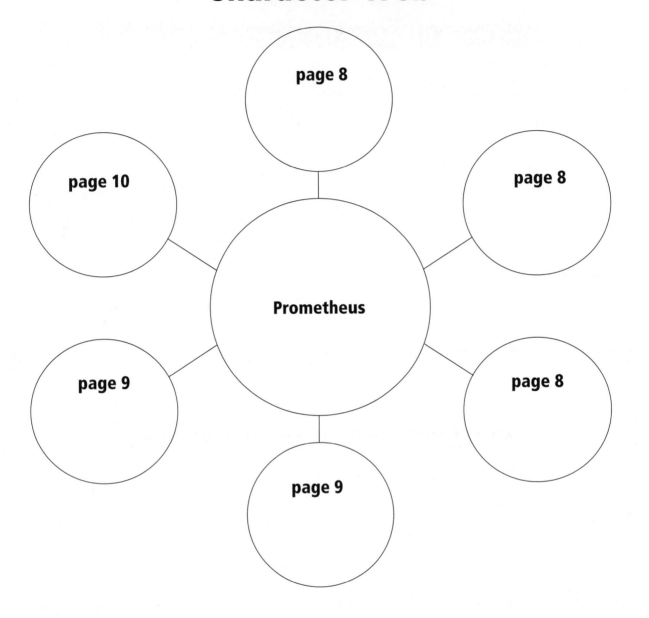

page 8

page 8

page 10

Prometheus

page 8

page 9

page 9

Prometheus is _____

but Zeus is _____

_____.

Name: _____

✏️ Close Reading Worksheet

First Read: Patterns across Cultures (orange boxes)

Page 16: This story is similar to "The Gift of Fire" because _____

_____

_____.

Page 19: There are three _____ and _____, and they are

important because _____.

Page 20: Like Prometheus, Coyote _____

_____,

but unlike Prometheus, Coyote _____.

Third Read: Critical Thinking (blue boxes)

Page 17: Coyote is smart to stay hidden and to watch the Skookums because

_____

_____.

Page 18: Based on how his sisters react, Coyote probably has _____

_____.

Support—Page 20: Coyote (is / is not) a trickster in this story because

_____

_____.

How Coyote Brought Fire to the Animal People Lesson 1 **225**

Name: _____

Plot Chart

Page 16: What happens first? (What is the problem?)

Page 17: What happens next?

Page 18: What happens after Coyote returns from the mountain?

Page 19: What is the first step in Coyote's plan to steal the fire?

Page 20: At the end of the story, how do Coyote and the other animals solve the problem of getting fire?

Name: _____

Compare and Contrast Chart

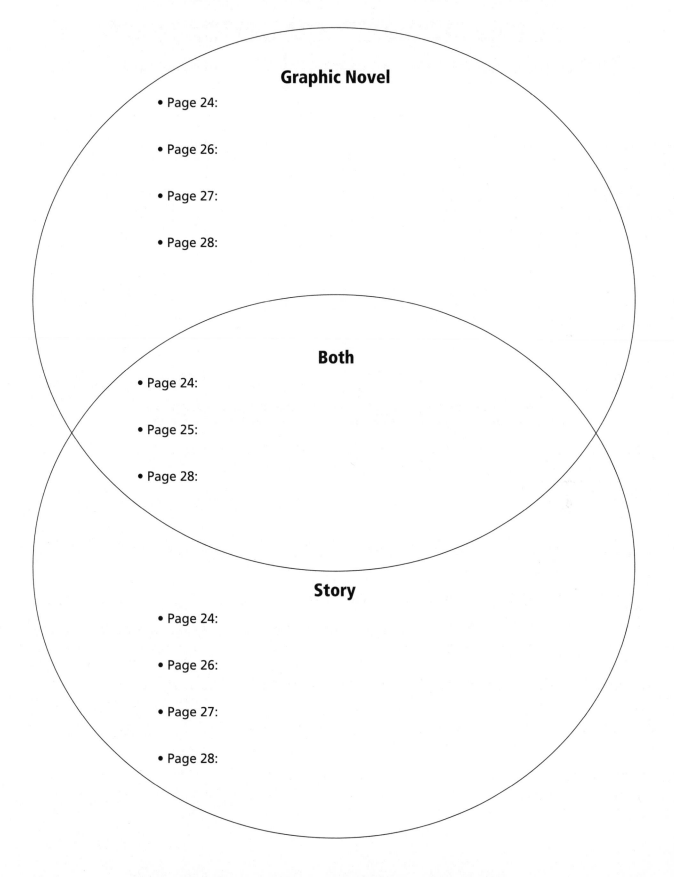

Graphic Novel

- Page 24:

- Page 26:

- Page 27:

- Page 28:

Both

- Page 24:

- Page 25:

- Page 28:

Story

- Page 24:

- Page 26:

- Page 27:

- Page 28:

How Coyote Stole Fire from the Skookums   Lesson 1   **227**

✎ Close Reading Worksheet

Second Read: Allusions to Mythology (green boxes)

Page 24: Squirrel probably considers Coyote to be a mentor because

_____

_____.

Page 25: I think Coyote's task could be described as Herculean because

_____

_____.

Page 26: The Skookums' Achilles' heel is _____

_____.

Third Read: Critical Thinking (blue boxes)

Page 26: Coyote says his thoughts aloud in the graphic novel version of the

story because _____

_____.

Page 27: In the graphic novel, there are three _____

_____.

Argue—Page 28: I think the animal people (would / would not) keep fire from

someone else who needed it because _____

_____.

Name: _____

✏️ Close Reading Worksheet

First Read: Draw Inferences (orange boxes)

Page 40: Zuri feels _____ about staying at her aunt's house

because _____

_____.

Page 41: Aunt Drusilla is _____

_____.

Page 43: I infer that Zuri is _____

_____.

Page 44: Zuri's mom got Zuri a puppy because _____

_____.

Third Read: Critical Thinking (blue boxes)

Page 42: The author includes this detail because _____

_____.

Page 43: Zuri uses a chess tip because _____

_____.

Compare—Page 44: Zuri's feelings have changed _____

_____

_____

_____.

Idioms, Adages, and Proverbs Chart

Idiom, Adage, or Proverb	What It Really Means
Page 40 Don't bite the hand that feeds you.	
Page 41 It's raining cats and dogs.	
Page 41 The early bird gets the worm.	
Page 42 Keep an eye on	
Page 42 Bite your tongue.	
Page 43 Nothing ventured, nothing gained	
Page 44 Let the cat out of the bag.	

Draw Conclusions Chart

Conclusion	Details That Support My Conclusion (Text Evidence and Prior Knowledge)
Page 48	
Page 49	
Page 50	
Page 51	
Page 52	

✏️ Close Reading Worksheet

Second Read: Point of View (green boxes)

Page 48: The words that tell who is speaking show that _____

_____ .

Page 49: _____ tells us about Rose's reaction. This shows the point

of view because _____

_____ .

Page 50: From the narrator's description, I learn that Jason is

_____

_____ .

Page 51: The story would be different if written from Christopher's first-person

point of view because _____ .

Third Read: Critical Thinking (blue boxes)

Page 50: When Tony says "what are friends for?" he means _____

_____ .

Page 50: Tony isn't talking with the other boys because _____

_____ .

Analyze—Page 52: The theme of this story is _____

_____ .

Name: _____

Make Predictions Chart

Page	My Prediction	Clues	What Actually Happened	Was I Correct?
64				
65				
67		1. 2.		

Name: _____

✏️ Close Reading Worksheet

Second Read: Elements of Drama (green boxes)

Page 64: Constance and Barnaby are _____. It says so in the

_____.

Page 64: Important details in the setting are _____

_____.

Page 66: The stage directions help me understand Holly's first line of dialogue

because _____.

Page 67: A new act begins on this page because _____

_____.

Third Read: Critical Thinking (blue boxes)

Page 66: The footprint will help Holly solve the mystery by _____

_____.

Page 67: In both cases, Mrs. Butterfield _____

_____.

Page 68: I think Cecily (does / does not) know what happened because _____

_____.

Analyze—Page 68: Mrs. Butterfield (does / does not) act like a guilty person because

_____

_____.

The Case of the Missing Ring

Name: _____

✏️ Close Reading Worksheet

First Read: Summarize (orange boxes)

Page 72: The most important idea is _____

_____.

Page 73: In scene 1, _____

_____.

Page 74: An important detail is that _____

_____.

Third Read: Critical Thinking (blue boxes)

Page 73: Mai-Lin becomes annoyed when _____

_____. She _____.

Page 74: _____acts most like a leader because _____

_____.

Page 76: The best problem solver is _____ because

_____.

For example, _____.

Compare and Contrast—Page 76: Mai-Lin's response was _____

_____. Kalisha's response was _____

_____. Both Mai-Lin and Kalisha _____

_____ , but _____

_____.

Name: _____

Character Motivation Chart

Page	Character	Character's Thoughts/Words/Actions	Character's Motivation
72	Kalisha		She wants to get everyone excited about how the money they raised will be used to paint a mural.
74	Mai-Lin		
75			This character wants to clear his or her name.
76	Kalisha		

The Money Goes Missing

Name: _____

Visualize Chart

Page 91

Page 93

Page 94

✏️ Close Reading Worksheet

Second Read: Elements of Poetry (green boxes)

Page 90: The rhyme pattern of the stanza is _____

_____.

Page 92: In this poem, the rhyme and the rhythm _____

_____.

Page 93: The rhythm of the poem is like the wind because _____

_____.

Third Read: Critical Thinking (blue boxes)

Page 90: The wind is upset at the moon because _____

_____.

Page 91: When the wind says he has knocked off the moon's edge, he means

_____

_____.

Page 93: I think the season of the poem is _____ because

_____.

Construct—Page 94: The wind (could / could not) make the moon disappear. The

last stanza tells me _____.

From this poem, I also learn that the moon _____

_____.

Name: _____

✏️ Close Reading Worksheet

First Read: Theme (orange boxes)

Page 99: The theme of the poem "The Wind Tapped Like a Tired Man" is

_____

_____ .

Page 100: The theme of "Winter" is _____

_____ .

Third Read: Critical Thinking (blue boxes)

Page 98: The poet feels _____ toward the wind because

_____ .

Page 99: The poet (has / has not) enjoyed her "visit" with the wind because

_____

_____ .

Compare—Page 100: Both poems say that nature is _____ . The poems

are different because _____

_____ .

Figurative Language Chart

Page 98

The Real Item	What the Poet Compares It To
wind	
wind	

Page 99

The Real Item	What the Poet Compares It To
wind's noise	
wind's noise	

Page 100

The Real Item	What the Poet Compares It To
robin's breast	
stars	

Name: _____

Main Idea and Details Chart

Main Idea

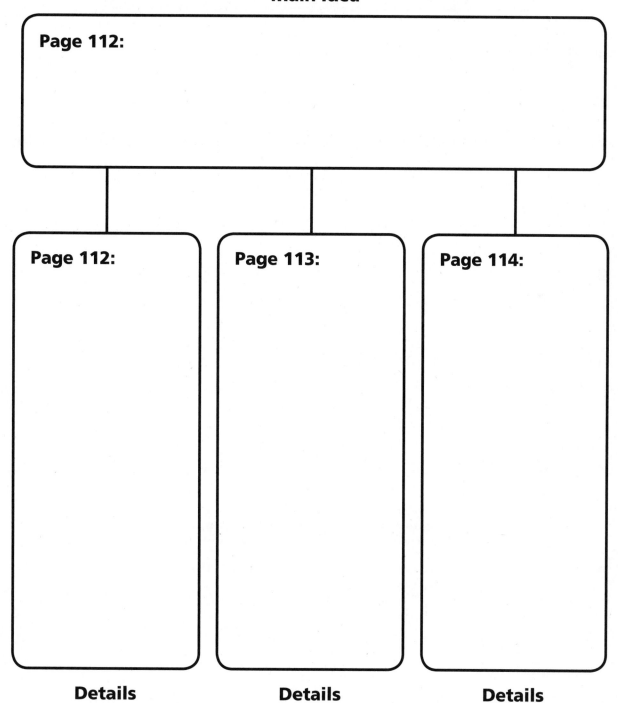

Page 112:

Page 112:

Page 113:

Page 114:

Details   **Details**   **Details**

Name: _____

✏️ Close Reading Worksheet

Second Read: Firsthand Account (green boxes)

Page 112: I know this is a firsthand account because _____

_____.

Page 113: The author might have gotten the number of deaths wrong because

_____

_____.

Page 114: The author's opinions about his fellow Chinese workers are _____

_____.

Page 116: The feelings or attitudes of _____

_____

would not appear in a secondhand account because _____

_____.

Third Read: Critical Thinking (blue boxes)

Page 115: The good things about camp life (did / did not) make up for the

hardships of railroad work because _____

_____.

Argue—Page 116: The building of a new national railroad (was / was not)
a good reason for the unfair treatment of the Chinese workers because

_____

_____.

Name: _____

Summary Chart

Page 120: How the Transcontinental Railroad Changed Travel

Page 121: The Race to Build the Transcontinental Railroad

Page 122: Finding Workers for the Central Pacific

Page 124: The Completion of the Transcontinental Railroad

Name: _____

✏️ Close Reading Worksheet

Second Read: Secondhand Account (green boxes)

Page 120: I know the article is a secondhand account because the writer says

_____

_____ .

Page 121: Some clues that tell me this is a secondhand account are _____

_____ .

Page 122: To get information, the author might have read such firsthand

accounts as _____

_____

_____ .

Page 123: The author probably learned that Crocker was proud of his workers by

_____

_____ .

Third Read: Critical Thinking (blue boxes)

Page 124: The completion of the transcontinental railroad was a historic moment

because _____

_____ .

Analyze—Page 124: The transcontinental railroad helped the United States by

_____

_____ .

Name: _____

✏️ Close Reading Worksheet

First Read: Cause and Effect (orange boxes)

Page 136: Coral reefs are favorite spots for ocean explorers because _____

_____ .

Page 138: Some people call coral reefs "rain forests of the sea" because _____

_____

_____ .

Page 139: Coral reefs absorb the force of waves and storms, which affects the

land by _____ .

Third Read: Critical Thinking (blue boxes)

Page 137: Corals need sunlight because _____

_____ .

Page 138: It is important for scientists to know when ocean temperatures or

chemical content change because _____

_____ .

Page 139: Coral reefs are major tourist attractions because _____

_____ .

Evaluate—Page 140: It is important to protect coral reefs because _____

_____

_____ .

Reasons and Evidence Chart

Idea	Reasons and Evidence That Support the Idea
Page 136: Corals are hunters, too.	
Page 138: Coral reefs are necessary for the health of the ocean.	
Page 139: Coral reefs are important to humans in many ways.	
Page 140:	Ten percent of coral reefs have been destroyed; many more face destruction over the next fifty years.

Name: _____

✏️ Close Reading Worksheet

First Read: Draw Conclusions (orange boxes)

Page 144: I conclude that most fish's bodies _____

_____ .

Page 145: I conclude that the life of a baby sea horse _____

_____ .

Page 146: I conclude that most other animals _____

_____ .

Page 147: I conclude that sea horses use camouflage because _____

_____ .

Third Read: Critical Thinking (blue boxes)

Page 144: I think this article is subtitled "Unique Creatures of the Sea" because

_____ .

Page 147: I think experts still have unanswered questions about sea horses

because _____

_____

_____ .

Analyze—Page 148: Protecting sea horses will help oceans because _____

_____

_____ .

Sea Horses: Unique Creatures of the Sea   Lesson 6   **247**

Cause-and-Effect Chart

Page 145

Causes
1.
2.

→

Effect
Many baby sea horses die before they reach adulthood.

Page 146

Cause

→

Effect/Cause
Food passes through its digestive system quickly.

→

Effect

Page 147

Cause

→

Effect/Cause
Sea horses are ripped loose from their anchors.

→

Effects
1.
2.

Page 148

Cause

→

Effect/Cause
Sea horses' habitat is destroyed.

→

Effect

Name: _____

Sequence Chart

Step 1, page 163

↓

Step 2, page 163

↓

Step 3, page 163

↓

Step 4, page 163

Name: _____

✏️ Close Reading Worksheet

Second Read: Diagrams (green boxes)

Page 161: The growths on right whales' heads are called _____.

Page 161: The _____ are at the tail end of the right whale.

Page 162: Lobster traps can harm a whale by _____

_____.

Third Read: Critical Thinking (blue boxes)

Page 160: People are the greatest threat to whales because _____

_____.

Page 161: Whale watching is a popular activity because _____

_____.

Page 164: Entanglement can be dangerous to rescuers when _____

_____.

Support—Page 164: The article supports the idea that solutions to big problems

require cooperation from many people _____

_____

_____.

Name: _____

Main Idea and Details Chart

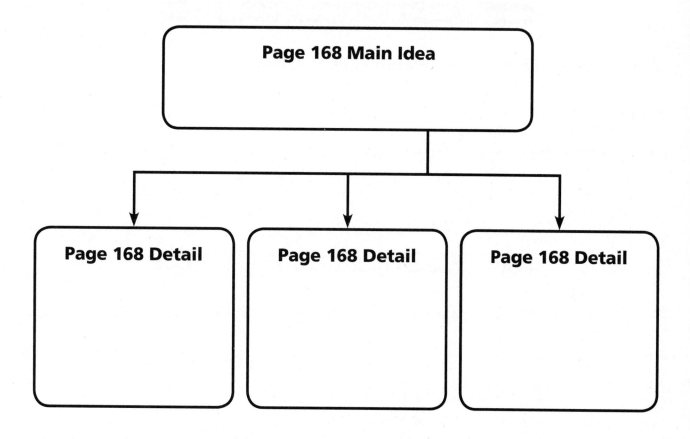

Page 168 Main Idea

Page 168 Detail

Page 168 Detail

Page 168 Detail

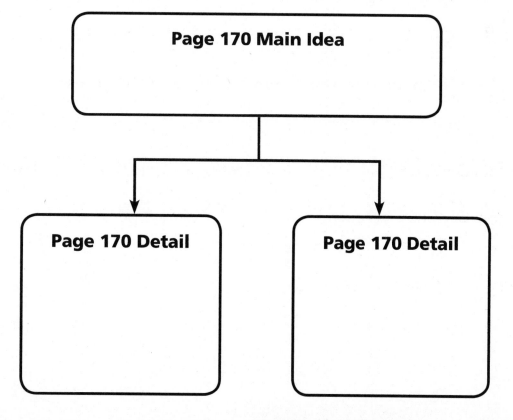

Page 170 Main Idea

Page 170 Detail

Page 170 Detail

Name: _____

✏️ Close Reading Worksheet

Second Read: Bar Graphs (green boxes)

Page 169: In 2012, _____ produced the greatest amount of maple syrup.

It produced _____ gallons.

Page 169: _____ and _____ both produced _____ thousand gallons.

Page 170: In _____, Wisconsin produced the fewest gallons of syrup.

Third Read: Critical Thinking (blue boxes)

Page 169: The 2011 season was great for syrup production because _____

_____.

Page 171: It is a good idea to cover the bucket _____

_____.

Page 172: You should refrigerate an open jar of maple syrup _____

_____.

Defend—Page 172: Having a successful maple syrup business depends on the

cooperation of nature because _____

_____.

✏️ **Close Reading Worksheet**

First Read: Paraphrase (orange boxes)

Page 176: Paraphase the third and fourth sentences in paragraph 2.

_____

_____.

Page 177: Paraphase the second and third sentences in paragraph 5.

_____

_____.

Page 180: Paraphrase the last two sentences of the article. _____

_____

_____.

Third Read: Critical Thinking (blue boxes)

Page 176: I think John Glenn got a tube of applesauce to eat on a space mission

because _____

_____.

Page 179: Tortillas help solve the crumb problem because _____

_____.

Apply—Page 180: In a low-gravity environment, I think it would be difficult to

_____

_____.

Name: _____

Problem-and-Solution Chart

Page 177:

Problem		Solution
Spaceships don't have refrigerators.	→	

Page 178:

Problem		Solution
Salt and pepper can fly into the air and cause problems for astronauts.	→	

Page 179:

Problem		Solution
Silverware floats in space.	→	

Page 180:

Problem		Solution
When Sandra cooks, foods and cooking tools float into space.	→	

Name: _____

Inferences Chart

Inference	Supporting Details from the Text
Page 194: Education played an important role in Lincoln's life.	
Page 195:	Edward's death was a great blow to Lincoln, but it would not be the only sad event in the future president's life.
Page 196: Lincoln's strong feelings against slavery led him to speak out, which made people see him as a good presidential candidate.	
Page 197: Lincoln wanted to free enslaved people.	
Page 198:	

✏️ Close Reading Worksheet

Second Read: Time Lines (green boxes)

Page 196: An event in Lincoln's early life that appears in the time line but not in

the text is _____.

Page 198: The event missing from the time line is _____

_____.

Page 198: The information that appears in the time line but not in the text is

_____.

Third Read: Critical Thinking (blue boxes)

Page 194: Holding many different jobs probably helped Lincoln by _____

_____

_____.

Page 195: Marrying an intelligent woman might have helped Lincoln because

_____.

Page 197: Some people told Lincoln to keep quiet about slavery because _____

_____.

Judge—Page 198: I think Lincoln (was / was not) a good president because

_____.

✏️ Close Reading Worksheet

First Read: Biography vs. Autobiography (orange boxes)

Page 202: I can tell the passage is (a biography / an autobiography) because

_____

_____ .

Page 205: The details that reveal the author's thoughts are _____

_____

_____ .

Page 206: The author probably shares her people's history with readers because

_____

_____ .

Third Read: Critical Thinking (blue boxes)

Page 202: The story starts at _____

because _____ .

Page 203: As an artistic child in a family that did not fully appreciate art,

Rebecca seems to have felt _____ .

Analyze—Page 206: Rebecca Fire Fox (would / would not) have felt proud of her

accomplishments without the award because _____

_____ .

Chronology Chart

Page 202–203: An Artist's Beginnings

Age 5:

Age 7:

↓

Page 204: My First Sculpture

Age 12:

↓

Page 205: Next Stop: Getting an Education

Age 14:

↓

Page 206: Returning Home and Becoming an Artist

Age 17:

Age 20: